KU-012-933

Contents

UNIVERSITY OXFORD COLLEGE

OXFORD

Preface

Classical Chinese architecture has undergone a long history of development, in the process acquiring a richly creative corpus of experience and achievement. The earliest buildings and building sites still in existence can be dated back as far as seven thousand years ago. Important examples of classical architecture run into the thousands; in Shanxi Province alone there are more than one hundred pre-14th century timber structures still in existence. World renowned masterpieces such as the Great Wall, the Zhaoxian stone bridge of the Sui Dynasty (581-618 A.D.), the palaces in Beijing of the Ming (1368-1644 A.D.) and Qing (1644-1911 A.D.) dynasties, and the private gardens of Suzhou have won unreserved admiration and praise from architects, archaeologists, artists, and men of letters both inside and outside China. Everyone finds the experience of roaming through the imperial palaces in Beijing and viewing the magnificent buildings to be most rewarding. Even the casual tourist would regret missing an opportunity to ascend the Great Wall for a sublime view of the country. The heritage of classical Chinese architecture, crystalizing the wisdom of her working people and produced as a collective effort among the brethren of her ethnic minorities, has long transcended mere national boundaries. It has become a treasure in the history of the world's architectural development.

Since the founding of the People's Republic of China, great attention has been given to the management of classical architecture as well as research on the subject. Many important historic buildings have been designated cultural artifacts with preservation priority, with reconstruction and repair initiated. Special research units have been formed to attend to historical documents on architecture, to prepare measured drawings of existing ancient buildings, and to study the subject of historical development.

With a view to passing on the heritage and furthering the development of Chinese architecture, we have collected and collated in this album valuable materials on the more important ancient building sites as well as famous classical buildings still in existence. Paintings and steles with architectural interest are also included. We hope that this album can give architects and researchers both inside China and abroad a vivid and concrete picture of classical Chinese architecture.

Included in this album are works of important architectural merit, as well as actual historical examples which embody significant development in building technology in the past. Materials were selected from all over the country. We have not only made a critical selection from already well known examples of historical architecture, but have also supplemented them with other significant examples discovered and excavated in recent years.

The majority of the plates included here, among which appear some rare items, are published for the first time. However, due to the lack of space, a large number of additional examples of classical architecture could not be included. Also omitted are certain aspects of this architecture which, though important, do not lend themselves to graphical representation. During the preparation of this album, we received assistance and support as well as relevant information from teams and individuals in the architectural profession, the press, and from the archaeological circle. For their cordial help and support, we wish to express here our heart-felt gratitude.

Chinese Academy of Architecture

June, 1979

Characteristics, History and Accomplishment of Ancient Chinese Architecture

Characteristics

Vast and populous, China is a great country with a long history and rich cultural traditions. She has a written history of about four thousand years, but the history of Chinese architecture goes back much further into antiquity. Architecture was born at the very dawn of civilization. Over long periods in history her working people, with wisdom and stamina, created a resplendent ancient culture, which included an architecture of unique historical style with many superb examples, be it of individual buildings, of composition in building ensembles, or of city planning. All have long been highly acclaimed and occupy an important place in the history of world architecture.

For several thousand years, ancient Chinese architecture has gone through a long and tortuous path. Nevertheless, it has managed to follow an unbroken line of development. Based on the needs of the people, and assimilating beneficial experiences and influences from various sources, it evolved independently with its own tenor from beginning to end. It is this very continuity, independence and adaptability that constitute the characteristics of the classical tradition.

Over 600,000 years ago, Peking Man, the distant ancestor of the Chinese race, was living on Chinese soil in a primitive society which lasted some several hundred thousand years. In the 21st century B.C., China entered into the period of caste society and the state appeared. In the following four thousand years, sixteen dynasties or periods succeeded each other. Yet for the greater part of the time, the country was a unified entity, in which culture was able to develop continuously. The country's unity lapsed only temporarily during the Spring and Autumn Period (770-476 B.C.), the Warring States Period (475-221 B.C.), the Period of the Three Kingdoms (220-280 A.D.), the period starting from the Eastern Jin to the Northern and Southern Dynasties (317-581 A.D.), the Period of the Five Dynasties and Ten States (907-960 A.D.) and the period of the Song, Liao, and Jin (960-1279 A.D.). Even during these periods, on the momentum of the nation's historical tradition, culture continued to evolve and flourish within the confines of each domain.

The Chinese nation is made up of over fifty different nationalities such as Han, Man, Mongol, Hui, Zang, Zhuang and Uygur. Chinese culture, with Han culture as its core, was created and enriched by all the nationalities working in concert. Political unity and the manifold bonds among the nationalities constituted a favorable condition for the continuity of ancient Chinese architecture. As one examines the evolution and transformation of Chinese architecture, one can clearly see a long line of development threading through from beginning to end. An architecture which has evolved continuously for several thousand years is rare in world history. Continuity can therefore be seen to be one of the distinguishing characteristics of classical Chinese architecture.

China is large in area. Its territory, comprising 9,600,000 square kilometers, stretches from 4°N to 53°N encompassing semi-tropical, temperate, and semi-arctic climates. Most of the country, however, lies in the temperate region. A mild climate, fertile soil, rich yields from the land, abundant forests and supplies of other building resources since ancient times constituted the material conditions suitable for independent economic development. Outside influences on indigenous Chinese culture were limited as there existed natural barriers in the form of oceans in the east and south, vast deserts to the north, and steep mountains to the west. Furthermore, centralized power in such a large nation naturally favored uniformity in administration, community structure, and production. These geographical and social factors determined Chinese architecture's unique characteristics in terms of style and paths of evolution. Such features as a structural system based on gracefully wrought timber, a meticulous and comprehensive scheme of city planning, a centralized national system of construction management, the rich and resplendent use of color and ornamentation on buildings, the salient style of garden design in the fashion of natural landscapes, and the arrangement and axial layout of buildings in conjunction with courtyards are distinctively Chinese. Uniqueness in style can therefore be said to be another characteristic of classical Chinese architecture.

Natural environments, however, differ from region to region, and encompass plains, plateaus, basins, grasslands, mountains, deserts, ridges and valleys. The economic life and customs also vary greatly among the different nationalities, placing tremendously divergent demands on architectural design. Furthermore, population in China grew rapidly in the span of several thousand years. From approximately 60,000,000 in the first century A.D., it increased to just below 100,000,000 in the twelfth century and reached 400,000,000 in the nineteenth century. The heavy demands that the expanding population made on architecture were many and varied. Unconfined and untrammeled by fixed methods and unafraid to innovate, Chinese workers in the past responded to given situations and dissimilar functional requirements by continually modifying previous architectural forms. Such aspects as structural systems, color and ornament, exterior design, etc., were all in a continuous process of transformation and improvement. For instance, even the roof bracket system, most characteristic of oriental architecture, reflects the typical stages of birth, evolution, improvement and metamorphosis. Change is therefore the third most important characteristic of classical Chinese architecture.

A Brief History

The development of classical architecture may be divided into five stages, each having its distinct, inherent characteristics.

Architecture of the Primitive Society Period

Primitive men, capable only of adaptation to natural conditions, chose to live in mountain caves close to water and hunting grounds. The natural caves in the vicinity of Zhoukoudian, in which Peking Man lived in communities some 400,000 to 500,000 years ago, are examples of these dwellings. In the south of China, which was damp and rampant with fierce animals, primitive men probably lived in trees.

Above 40,000 years ago, primitive society in China gradually evolved into matriarchal clan communities. Later, about 6,000 to 7,000 years ago when matriarchal clan communities prevailed and agriculture was practised, people began to make dwellings by digging pits which they covered with simple timber roofs. These in turn formed the villages. In such a way, the construction activities of man began. Primitive clan communal villages appeared in large numbers along the Yellow River Basin because of the favorable natural conditions there. Typical examples are found in the archaeological sites at Banpo (near Xi'an, Shaanxi Province) and Jiangzhai (in Lintong, Shaanxi). In plan, these dwellings were either quadrangular or circular with a diameter of about four meters, either half-sunk or entirely subterranean. They all face a communal square, while kilns and graves were scattered about in separate plots.

About 5,000 years ago, matriarchal clan communities along the Yellow River and Yangtze River had, one after the other, evolved into patriarchal clan communities. At this time, some of the constructed dwellings were set up entirely on the surface of the ground. Besides circular and quadrangular forms, there were also plans in the form of the Chinese character 吕 . In addition, dwellings were sometimes constructed in such a way that three to five cubicles were joined together in a row. In other regions, due to dissimilar geographical and climatic conditions, buildings of many diverse forms of construction appeared. In the riparian regions in the South, dwellings were constructed over closely spaced stilts. In the vicinity of Jiangxi, houses were built with inverted trapezoidal roofs with a long ridge and short curves. In Inner Mongolia small round huts were built with stones. Structurally, houses in the North basically consisted of overlapping wooden members fastened with rope or ratten strips. In the South, primitive wood-jointing techniques appeared, along with grass sod roofing and timber studed earth walls.

Architecture of the Slave Society Period

This period lasted approximately 1,600 years from the 21st century B.C. to 476 B.C. Ancient legends as recorded in historical chronicles indicate that China entered the period of slave society from the beginning of the Xia Dynasty. Repair and construction work on city walls, moats and palaces took place in the Xia Dynasty. Yu, the founder of Xia, mobilized a gigantic labor force to maintain canals, control floods, and dig watercourses for irrigation. However, architectural remains that belong unequivocally to the Xia Dynasty have yet to be discovered.

Slave society in China reached its maturity in the Shang Dynasty in the 17th century B.C. when slavery was exploited on a large scale by the rulers, resulting in the creation of the resplendent Bronze Age. Subsequently, bronze tools replaced stone tools, and based on some traces of ancient architecture, we may concluded that the saw was in use. Capitals of the Shang Dynasty were all surrounded with lofty city walls, and inside the walls were compounds of palaces, gardens and pools. From the extant archaeological examples of the early Shang palaces in Erlitou (in Yanshi, Henan Province) and mid-Shang palaces in Panlongcheng (in Huangpo, Hubei Province), we can safely say that by that time a higher level of building techniques had evolved. Believing in ''reverence for the gods and service for the ghosts'', the slave owner demanded burial in tombs, the construction of which consequently became a major building activity at that time. In a late Shang capital site at Xiaotun (in Anyang, Henan Province), there were extensive building sites for palaces and ancestral halls and more than ten large tombs inside the burial ground. These tombs had hundreds of human sacrificial burial victims. Tomb caves were built as deep down as thirteen meters underground. In the center, huge logs were piled to form funerary chambers. Furthermore, rammed earth with formwork construction, an innovation at that time, was widely used in the construction of city walls, high terraces and podia for buildings. Extant city walls of the Shang Dynasty at Zhengzhou were built in layers to a thickness of seven to ten centimeters. Each layer was rammed evenly. This shows that earth-ramming

technique had matured. The combined use of earth and wood widened the scope of arthitecture, so much so that the term ''tumu'' (meaning earth and wood) was in ancient times a synonym for building construction.

The Zhou Dynasty, established in the 11th century B.C., inherited and further developed the Shang culture. The capital was built at Gaojing (southwest of present-day Xi'an in Shaanxi Province), and the East Capital was built at Luoyi (present-day Luoyang, Henan Province). Members of the royal family and the aristocracy were granted land on which they could set up their feudal states in various parts of the country. As a result, building activities increased. From the excavation of the early Western Zhou (1066-771 B.C.) palace sites at Qishan we can see that a pattern of building had already taken shape which combined a royal court in the front with an imperial household to the rear, replete with a system of porches. Individual buildings had regularly spaced columns and evenly distributed bays, utilizing rammed earth walls. From details of bronze vessels we can see the use of corbel brackets (dou) on column heads, as well as horizontal cantilever railings. Roofing construction improved with the advent of earthenware tiles at that time.

After 770 B.C. much social turmoil occurred in the Spring and Autumn Period. For self defense in their constant fighting against each other, feudal lords, weak or strong, all resorted to building fortresses which thus became a common category of construction engineering of that era. Also, the constant accumulation of wealth in towns placed higher functional demands on architecture. The application of coloring, carving and other ornaments on buildings had already begun, as indicated by the use of such terms as ''carved hills on the pillars and duckweed on the joints'' (shanjie zaozhuo), ''red columns'' (danying), ''colorful rafters'' (caichuan) and ''carved laths'' (kejue) in literary documents describing architectural exteriors.

Architecture of the Early Feudal Period

Architecture of this phase underwent evolutionary development over a period of more than 1,000 years, from the beginning of the Warring States Period to the period of the Northern and Southern Dynasties, i.e. from 475 B.C. to 581 A.D. During this era, feudal society became firmly established and strong. At the time of Han Dynasty (206 B.C. to 220 A.D.), the replacement of bronze vessels by iron vessels had been completed, and the system of timber frame construction had assumed its initial form.

In the Spring and Autumn Period, there were some one hundred and forty states. As a result of conquests and annexations, however, only seven large states among them survived to enter the Warring States Period. These seven states were Qi, Chu, Yan, Han, Zhao, Wei and Qin. The capitals and commercial towns of these states enjoyed unprecedented prosperity. Linzi of Qi, Handan of Zhao, Chengzhou of Zhou, Daliang of Wei, Yanying of Chu and Yiyang of Han were all large, populous towns with handicraft industry and commercial concentrations. Situated within these towns were palaces, government offices, workshops and markets. The construction of elevated terraces also became popular at this time, as the rulers of each state used ''lofty terraces and magnificent palaces'' to flaunt their wealth and power and to ''preen themselves''.

In 221 B.C., the First Emperor of Qin, by conquering the other six states, founded the first centralized feudal empire in China. Building activities of yet larger scale began. Roads were improved, the great canal of Honggou was excavated, the grand waterway of Lingqu was dug, and the Great Wall was built. Over seven hundred thousand conscripts were deployed in the refurbishing and building of the gigantic and extravagant Epang Palaces and the Lishan Mausoleum. Skilled craftsmen and superior materials, drawn from all over the country, were mobilized for the erection of palace buildings on the high grounds north of Xianyang after the style of the palaces of the six defeated states. Within two hundred miles of the capital alone, two hundred and seventy detached palaces and royal residences were constructed.

After the Qin, the Western Han (206 B.C. to 23 A.D.) and Eastern Han (25 A.D. to 220 A.D.) further developed the feudal economy and opened the Silk Route, the thoroughfare of East-West trade and cultural exchange. Han capital cities were still more grand in scale; their palaces and gardens were yet more splendid. The Weiyang and Changluo palaces in Chang'an (present-day Xi'an, Shaanxi Province) were both large building ensembles of some ten kilometers in perimeter. The north-south throughway in that city was five and a half kilometers long, fifty meters wide, and flanked by trees on both sides. Inside the city, there were nine marketplaces. At the time of Emperor Han Wu Di, "the one hundred schools were abolished and Confucianism was exclusively respected". The Confucian teaching of "reverence for the deceased and remembrance of the past" strengthened the elaborate funerary system in practice since Shang times, causing the physical standards of royal tombs to rise yet higher. Since the Eastern Han the traditional practice of using timber for tombs was abandoned. In place of timber, bricks and stones were employed for the construction of funerary chambers. The wealth of architectural forms and expression during the Han is reflected in the above-ground stones of extant mausoleums, the burial earthenwares inside the tombs, and the ornamental frescos and brick and stone reliefs on the tomb walls.

During the Western and Eastern Han Dynasties socio-economic development in feudal China reached its first climax. Changes in technology and the art of building created a new epoch. No longer confined to single story structures, timber framing technology reached a higher plane and began to be used in the construction of upper stories. Five basic roof forms emerged, namely the *wudian* (hipped roof), *xuanshan* (roof with gabled ends which have purlins projecting out to support 5 to 8 rafters), *dunding* (slightly vault-shaped roof), *zuanjian* (pointed roof) and *xieshan* (half-hipped, half-gabled roof). More extensive use of bricks, stone and lime began, reflecting more varied and specialised applications. For example, hollow bricks with a length of one and a half meters were used in tombs; small-scaled, wedge-shaped, and notched bricks were used in vault construction. Eave-end tiles added a rich variety of patterns. Indeed, decorative patterns in great profusion were applied to floor tiles, beams, columns, corbel brackets, doors and windows, walls, ceilings and rooftops by means of color painting, carving, or modeling.

Towards the end of the Eastern Han, fighting among warlords ended up in a situation leaving the three kingdoms of Wei, Shu and Wu opposing each other. A short period of unification occurred when Western Jin conquered Wu in 280 A.D. Fighting among the ruling classes for power and control soon developed. Taking advantage of these conflicts, the upper strata of the Huns, Xianbeis, Jies, Dis, Jiangs and other nationalities which then inhabited the western and northern areas formed separate political factions and established sixteen states between 304 A.D. and 460 A.D. This period is referred to in historical chronicles as the Sixteen States. It was not until 439 A.D. when Northern Wei destroyed Northern Liang that North China became unified. The Northern and Southern Dynasties Period, in which the South and the North opposed each other, began in the year 420 A.D. when Emperor Wu (Liu Yu) established the Song Dynasty (to make a distinction from the Song Dynasty established in 960 A.D., this dynasty of Liu Yu is often referred to by historians as the Liu Song Dynasty) after having wrested political power from Eastern Jin in the south. Decades of warfare imposed great suffering and hardship on the lives of the people. It was at this time that Buddhism, which had been making inroads into China since the Eastern Han, was advocated by the ruling class and flourished. The extensive construction of Buddhist temples and pagodas thus became a major building activity of this period, apart from the building of towns and palaces. Within the Northern Wei territory, over thirty thousand Buddhish temples were built. In its capital of Luoyang alone, there were one thousand three hundred and sixty-seven temples. Jiankang, capital of the Southern dynasties, had over five hundred. The Yongling Monastery in Luoyang as recorded in the *Luoyang Qielan Ji* (*A Record of Buddhist Temples in Luoyang*) was a large monastery with nine-storied timber pagoda which was "visible a hundred miles away from the capital". This tall and large wooden structure was representative of the level of building construction in that period. Besides these, grottoes and frescos were constructed along the contours of hills. Famous examples include those at Yungang (in Datong, Shaanxi Province), Longmen (in Luoyang, Henan Province), Mogao (in Dunhuang, Gansu Province), Maiji Mountain (in Tianshui, Gansu Province), Tianlong Mountain (in Taiyuan, Gansu Province) and Xiangtang Mountain (in Handan, Hebei Province). In precise and minute strokes, the masons carved out not only enormous Buddhist effigies, but also imitations of timber corridor construction, thus preserving images of the contemporary building art.

A study of the ceilings of these grotoes reveals the numerous forms of ceiling construction of that period. The inverted bucket form, the octagonal form, the flat chessboard top, and the pyramidal lotus top are just a few examples. The use of glazed tiles in important buildings had also begun in the Period of the Northern and Southern Dynasties.

Architecture of the Middle Feudal Period

Commencing with the Sui Dynasty, continuing through the Tang and Song and ending with the period of the Liao, Jin and Yuan (i.e. from 581 A.D. to 1368 A.D.), this epoch covers seven to eight hundred years. In this era, building technology matured further, methodical design for timber structures came into use, and the organization and management of building construction became more thorough. Many extant historical buildings serve as examples in our analysis of the architectural development of this period.

The split between the south and the north which lasted for three and a half centuries finally ended with the advent of the Sui Dynasty. During that short dynasty, the famous Dayunhe (Great Canal) was dug. Running from Hangzhou in the south to Zhuojun in the north, it had a length of 1790 kilometers. A large number of extravagant palaces and parks were built in Chang'an, Luoyang, Jiangdu and other locations.

The Tang Dynasty, founded in 618 A.D., was a gloriously resplendent period in the history of Chinese feudal society. This dynasty saw highly developed crafts and trade, unprecedented urban prosperity both inland and along the coast, and generations of literary and artistic geniuses such as the poets Li Bai and Du Fu, the painter Wu Daozi, the sculptor Yang Weizhi, and men of letters such as Han Yu and Liu Zhongyuan. Tang architecture, which collectively reflected contemporary politics, economics, and culture, also displayed new achievements. On the foundations of the Sui city of Daxing was built the world's then greatest, most meticulously planned capital city, Chang'an (present-day Xi'an in Shaanxi Province). On over eight thousand hectares of land, all kinds of structures and facilities such as palaces, government offices, residential compounds, markets, temples, greenbelts and drainage systems were laid out according to plan; well differentiated major and secondary roads formed a rectilinear and disciplined system. Furthermore, Tang architecture was exceptionally grand and ornate. As recorded in historical chronicles, hugh edifices such as *mingtang* (imperial lecture and ceremonial hall — the particular *mingtang* referred to here was the Wanxiang Shengong) and *tiantang* were built at Luoyang. The magnificence of Tang architecture is also born out by findings at the sites of the Hanyuan and Linde palaces which were excavated in recent years. The existing Foguang Temple at Wutai, Shanxi Province, is a large hall of seven bays whose column spacing in plan fitted the needs of a Buddhist hall and whose corbel brackets were securely fastened to the beams. Still standing proudly as a lone survivor after a thousand years, this building testifies to the level of Tang structural technology in timber. Other innovations were found in pagoda, tomb, and bridge works. These achievements of Tang building not only helped architecture in central China to prosper, but also exerted a widespread influence to outlying districts as far away as Xinjiang, Tibet, and Heilongjiang.

In 906 A.D. the Tang Dynasty collapsed, and China plunged once again into political disunity with "five dynasties and ten states". This fragmentation lasted in the central plains and southern districts until 960 A.D., when they were united under the Song, and in the north until 1280 A.D., when China was once more unified, this time under Kublai Khan who founded the Yuan Dynasty after the passage of the Liao, Western Xia and Jin dynasties.

Handicraft industry flourished in the Northern Song Dynasty, and new progress was made in ceramics, paper-making, textiles, printing and ship-building. Gun powder and movable block printing also were invented. Trade grew rapidly. The capital, Bianjing (present-day Kaifeng), was not only a political center, but also a commercial metropolis. The thousand-year-old urban system whereby centralized markets and zones of residences were enclosed by high walls and locked up at night was abolished. The walls were demolished, curfew was lifted, and shops grouped according to their trades lined the streets. Tea houses, restaurants, inns, theatres and other public buildings appeared in profusion. The unfolding city life brought a new face to the urban centers. Artistry on buildings of this period became richer and more polychromatic, with a higher level of workmanship in the artistic use of glazes, color painting and decorative joinery. Glazed tiles of a golden yellow color were used in large quantities when the palace buildings in Zhongdu (present-day Beijing) were built in the Jin Dynasty (1115-1234 A.D.). Also during this time, glazed wall tiles of various colors were used on some important buildings. Colorful lacquer paints were applied liberally to wood frame members in both interiors and on the outside. As early as the Northern Song there were already five standardized motifs in official color-painted decorations. The ancient custom of sitting on floor mats underwent change during the Tang Dynasty, and became completely replaced by raised seating in the Song Dynasty. Subsequently, indoor furniture such as the bedtable gave way to higher tables and chairs. Doors and windows generally became openable leaves, fitted with window traceries with many kinds of gydangea and hyacinth flower patterns. The style of Song architecture as a whole presents a flamboyant and exquisite image. The Liao Dynasty to the north, on the other hand, adhered more to the Tang tradition; the well-known Muta (Wooden Pagoda) in Yingxian County and the Guanyin Pavilion at Dule Temple, Jixian County, retained the former style of structural discipline and masculine grandeur.

Architecturally, the Northern Song legacy to prosterity also includes a book devoted to building construction, namely the *Yingzao Fashi (Treatise on Architectural Methods)* published in 1103. Compiled by Li Jie, this was a manual of national building standards, containing detailed design principles of thirteen types of buildings, their modular dimensions, their construction methods, material quantities, and design patterns. Rules and techniques for the construction of each building and each component were set down after the material, structural and aesthetic factors had been analysed. The principle of modular dimensioning was thus expounded and its flexible application given consideration. This book is not only a rare literary source on classical Chinese architecture, but is also a summation of building technology of the middle period of the feudal society.

After the Yuan unification of China, its capital was built at Dadu (present-day Beijing). As a governing artifice for the ruler, various religions were advocated, among which Buddhism and Lamaism occupied a special place. Consequently, Lamaist temples and Tibetan styled vase-shaped pagodas were built everywhere in Central China, and foreign influence on architectural ornamentation was experienced. In terms of China's cultural development, the Yuan opera represented a climax in its own right. Architecturally, it stimulated the extensive erection of a new building type — the theatres — among the people.

Architecture of the Late Feudal Period

This phase corresponds with the Ming and Qing dynasties. During the five hundred years from 1368 to the Opium War in 1840, agriculture and handicraft industry reached the highest attainable level of feudal society. The capacity for political unity within the feudal system was realised, and the Chinese people advanced one more step towards integration and consolidation. The unity of the country promoted cultural exchange between the North and the South, and among all the nationalities. Architecture continued to make progress, and achieved outstanding success, especially in garden making and architectural ornamentation. Brick construction technology advanced rapidly during the Ming Dynasty. As a result, most city walls were laid with brick and many "beamless" great halls were built with brick vaulting. This period also saw the building of quite a few defense towns along the coast, and the further reconstruction of the world-famous Great Wall.

The Ming Dynasty built its capital in Nanjing at first but moved it later at the beginning of the fifteenth century to Beijing. There, renovation and expansion transformed the former Yuan capital into the famous historic city of the late feudal period. The glorious and opulent Zijincheng (Forbidden City) constituted the city center. This was a full realization of the "palace-as-nucleus" city planning concept found in ancient chronicles. Consistent with this concept, a central axis, some eight kilometers long, penetrates the entire city. Along this axis, city gates, squares, watch towers, palaces, artificial hills and pavilions were built. Rising and falling, they formed a disciplined composition of dynamic and powerful grandeur. The art of composing architectural ensembles in the feudal era had reached its zenith.

The mausoleums of the Ming emperors were sited at Changping, Beijing, and surrounded by mountains. The entrance to the royal necropolis is flanked by two knolls on either side. Following the topography inside the valley, thirteen royal mausoleums were laid out. A seven-kilometer tomb passage leads into the necropolis ensemble. The marvelous harmony between architecture and topography produces a solemn and dignified atmosphere for the funerary park.

The political system and cultural life of the Qing Dynasty were basically the same as that of the Ming. Architecture, likewise, followed the same lineage without any conspicuous divergence. The art of garden-making attained epochal success. Within two hundred years or so, the aristocracy had built a large number of gardens such as Yuan Ming, Yihe (Summer Palace), and Jingming in the western outskirts of Beijing, and had also completed the three city lakes at Xi Yuan begun in the Ming, namely Beihai, Zhonghai, and Nanhai. In the reigns of emperors Kang Xi and Qian Long, large-scale summer resorts were built at Chengde outside the Great Wall. During the two dynasties of Ming and Qing, the rich and powerful constructed their private gardens mostly in the regions around Suzhou, Hangzhou, Wuxi and Yangzhou south of the Yangtze River. The vogue of garden-making was at its peak. These gardens, embodying the rich experiences of the past, fully manifested the unique characteristics of the Chinese landscape garden. The creation of a rich array of imageries and aesthetic concepts established Qing gardens as a unique school among the world tradition of landscape architecture.

As the Qing rulers continued to exploit religion as a means to control their subjects, Lamaist temples were built extensively in all regions of the minority nationalities. The Drepung Monastery in Tibet, the Kumbum Monastery in Qinghai Province, and the Labrang Monastery in Gansu Province are all famous examples rich in the cultural characteristics of the nationalities. The Potala Palace in Lhasa, Tibet, built in the early seventeenth century, perched on top of a precipitous cliff, and seemingly integral with the mountain peaks, constituted a novel architectural form. The Waiba Temples in Chengde were a series of architectural creations which amalgamated the individual styles of the Tibetan, Mongolian and Han nationalities into one entity.

In Qing timber construction technique, extensive use was made of fastening and jointing methods to fabricate large structural members with small units. By this means, an alternative method of building large structures was introduced. New levels were reached in the techniques of glazing and glass firing, resulting in changes in the coloration of building exteriors. During this period, all sorts of refined arts and crafts, such as gold plating, gilding, inlay work, carving and lacquering were utilized along with silk tapestries and scroll paintings in architectural ornamentation. In combination with traditional methods such as color painting, glazing, plastering and wall papering, these techniques cosmeticised classical architecture into something yet more polychromatic, exquisite and stylish.

After the middle of the Qing Dynasty, the feudal system approached the brink of disastrous collapse. Waves of peasant revolts, rising and falling, began to undermine Qing rule. The Opium War, which broke out between China and Britain in 1840, virtually proclaimed the dissolution of China's feudal system, and ushered in a period of semi-feudal, semi-colonial society. As this was happening, modern Chinese architecture, a new chapter in the development of China's heritage, began to take its shape.

Achievements in Technology and Art

Born of an independent society and its own indigenous environment, classical Chinese architecture has, over several thousand years, grown into a complete and independent system whose legacy has greatly enriched the world's architectural heritage. This system encompasses many aspects, from the layout of cities to the composition of architectural ensembles, from construction methods to color ornamentation, from exterior form to interior decoration and furnishing, and from building technology to architectural art. We may begin to explore the achievements in the art and science of this system of architecture by examining the following aspects:

The Early Establishment of a Town Planning Theory and Its Large Scale Implementation

In *Kao Gong Ji* (*The Artificers' Record*), completed during the Period of Warring States in the fifth century A.D., mention is made of canons for the laying out of the royal city — the capital and seat of the emperor. This is the earliest written theory known on planning. According to this document, the capital city was to be nine square *li* (one *li* was about 400 meters) in area. There should be three gates on each side and the width of the main thoroughfare leading from the principal city gate is to be nine cart lanes abreast. The palace itself should be at the center of the capital, with the imperial court in the front, the market to the rear, and a place for worshipping the deity of the locality on the right. This complete concept has been followed as a model by successive generations of rulers in their building of capital cities; it was implemented authentically in the layouts of Yuan and Ming Beijing. In *Guan Zi*, another book completed during the Warring States Period, quite a few principles of site selection for a city are given. For instance, according to the book, a city should be divided into neighborhood units, and should be zoned according to professions and trades.

Subsequently, in a China studded with cities, these principles found not infrequent application. Qin Xianyang, built between the fourth and third century B.C., and Han Chang'an are fine examples of their full application. Both Xianyang and Chang'an were on high ground on either side of the River Wei in the Guangzhong region, thus gaining easy access to water while avoiding flood hazards. On the east side, water transport was facilitated by other rivers such as Jing, Qing, Luo and Ba. Via their confluence with the River Wei, they connected the metropolises with the Yellow River which flowed thence eastward to the central plains. Within the boundary of Guanzhong stretched a thousand miles of fertile land which yielded abundant agricultural products. The bountiful Sichuan to the south provided the capital with ample supplies of food and clothing. In terms of military logistics the location permitted "controlling Yao-Han to the east with the left arm; embracing Long-Shu to the southwest with the right". The direction of the rivers' flow facilitated military advance, while the ridges permitted defense. In these examples of capital-building and military control, such siting criteria were indeed very meticuously applied.

Chao Cuo of the Han Dynasty in the second century B.C. had proposed the ideas of stabilizing the borders through settlement, and of planning these border cities. He concluded that the location of a city must take into account linkage to navigable waters, rich vegetation and fertile soils. Each city was to have a thousand households, organized into residential quarters, and each house would consist of three connected buildings. Roads linking these to farmed fields must be developed beforehand. Also needed early would be physicians to treat the sick and priests to officiate at religious rituals, as well as afforestation and the laying out of burial grounds. Numerous military town sites excavated in recent years in Inner Mongolia and on either side of the section of the Great Wall in Gansu Province demonstrate that these proposals had in fact been extensively adopted.

Chang'an, the capital of the Sui and Tang dynasties in the sixth century A.D., is yet another full implementation of city planning on a large scale. The ordering of its zones, circulation network, residential districts, palaces and markets represent the culmination of city-making endeavours up to that time. The city had an orderly grid system of roads, with a 150-meter wide major thoroughfare. The palace and government offices were situated in the north of the city, from which the main street of Zhuquedajie led straight to the south gate of the city. The east and west sides of the city were each provided with a market. The city was subdivided into 108 residential quadrangles, with boundary walls surrounding each. The northwest outskirts were the imperial scenic region. For the enjoyment of the common people, the northeast corner had been developed into the Qujiang Pond and the Furong Garden. Inside the city, there were four nullahs on top of a conduit which conducted water specifically to the palace compound. Main thoroughfares were all lined with cultivated trees. This typical city of feudal China was the world's largest planned city at the time. The influence of its planning concepts and layout configuration was very widespread, reaching as far as Japan across the seas.

The layout of Suzhou (known as Pingjiang Prefecture in Song times), a city reputed to be the Venice of the East, reflects another adaptive planning approach. Taking advantage of the bountiful surface water resources in that city, a network of canals was formed consisting of a moat around the city, a main canal, and street canals within the city. This provided for drainage as well as for transport. The houses all faced a street in the front and abutted on a canal in the back, forming a city of water hamlets with a unique scenic charm.

The utilization of the water element in the capital of Dadu in the Yuan Dynasty was equally successful in aspects of its planning and design. There, the inflow from various tributaries of Xishan (West Mountain) was diverted into artificial ponds and lakes within and around the city before discharging eastwards into the Grand Canal. This arrangement catered at once for the needs of both water supply and water transport for the city, and embellished it with delightful waterscapes as well — another successful piece of planning and design.

The Innovation of a Highly Adaptable System of Timber Construction and Its Continual Development and Improvement

Timber has been the basic structural material in Chinese classical architecture. The beams-in-tiers method constitutes its major framing system. With this method, columns support beams, which in turn support other tiers of beams on top. Purlins are supported at the ends of these beams. Besides this method, purlins may rest directly on columns, or on short piers supported by beams, the columns and short piers being mortised for jointing with beams, forming a column-and-tie-beam structural system. Or logs may be stacked up as walls to form a quadrangular enclosure in a log-cabin type of construction. In yet another mode of construction, raised dwellings are built with their floordecks supported on stilts. Such a diverse system of timber construction has proved to be flexible enough to meet the functional and aesthetic requirements of various building types from small domestic buildings and garden structures to large palaces, temples, bridges, workshops, and tall pagodas and towers.

Many fine examples of world famous timber structures are still extant, such as the main hall of Foguang Temple built in Tang times one thousand one hundred years ago, the Guanyin Pavilion of Dule Temple built one thousand years ago, the 66-meter high Śākyamuni Pagoda of Fogong Temple built nine hundred years ago, and the Ling'en Temple in the mausoleum of Chang Ling of the Ming Dynasty (the largest extant hall from the past, with a floor area close to two thousand square meters, built five hundred years ago). As to the front hall of the Qin Epang Palace which "seats ten thousand persons and stands five *zhang* high banners indoors (about 14 meters)", the 100-meter high Wooden Pagoda at the Yongling Temple in Luoyang in Northern Wei times, and other such buildings described in historical records, one cannot help marveling at the stupendous scale of their construction.

The design flexibility of this timber structural system may be attributed to its several inherent advantages. Firstly, its column grid can be varied, allowing omission or shifting of column supports in planning; the width of the bays and floor heights are also variable to satisfy different functional demands. Secondly, its use is not confined to single story buildings, but is adaptable for multi-storied structures as well. Thirdly, because of its frame construction, its perimeter enclosures can be freely located, varied in thickness, and may be either enclosed or open. Because of its high adaptability, this system has continued to be useful for several thousand years throughout the

long history of Chinese architecture. Such 'longevity' is rare among structural systems anywhere in the world.

In response to new functional requirements, Chinese timber construction of the past never stopped undergoing innovation and improvement. This factor ensures its persistence and relevance. We need only look back briefly at its history to discover the lineage of its evolution.

In primitive society, structural wood members were fastened together, and the ends of posts were buried in the ground. However, no later than in the slave society, tenon jointing began to be used in roof construction. By the Han Dynasty, the placing of columns on bases on the ground completely replaced the earlier practice of burying their bottom ends in the ground. At the same time, the superstructure consisted of an integral and rigid framework, and included corbel brackets (*dougong*) which supported projecting eave components. Nevertheless, large buildings still relied on rammed earth walls and pounded earth podia for stability, resulting in what actually were composite wood-and-earth structures. From the Northern and Southern Dynasties to Sui and Tang, augmenting earth walls were dispensed with in favor of entirely timber designs; brackets and the overall timber framework were integrated as mutually strengthening components of one integral whole. Progress in structural form continued during the two Song, the Jin and the Yuan dynasties. In Ming and Qing times, the shortage of timber led to the technique of jointing and paneling, whereby tall columns and large beams could be fabricated by jointing small-size stock. Beams and columns were connected together directly, thus simplifying the overall structure and freeing the interior frame from restrictions imposed by brackets, which were now relegated to decorative adjuncts on the external eaves.

Today, thanks to the progress made in construction materials and techniques ancient wood framing methods are no longer important for practical construction. However, the knowledge of the structural principles of this extremely adaptable system of timber frame construction, as well as its ever-evolving, ever-developing standards, continues to inspire us.

The Creation of an Architecture with Distinctive National Characteristics and Styles

The creativity of classical Chinese architecture has left us with a valuable legacy in terms of form, color, ornamentation, and the ordering of space. Some of the concepts and methods, nurtured over long periods of time in the living environments of the people, and thus imbued with strong national characteristics and distinctive styles, have wide and universal appeal.

A major trait of this classical architecture is its exquisite integration of artistry and function, materials and structure. Beauty becomes something inherent. To give but a few examples of the components that manifest this characteristic, raised terraces guard against dampness, large eave overhangs shelter against rain, lattice on windows and doors facilitate the mounting of paper to admit light, and decorated tiles are an integral component of roofing materials. Decorated corbel brackets, architrave tie ends, steps and door nail studs are all functional components of the structure and not just superfluous adjuncts. Even the painted frieze, so full of decorative intentions, originated out of the need to preserve timber by the application of paint. Art work popularly used in secular buildings such as stucco, ridge tiles, lattice work on windows and screen walls all reflect the materials and underlying structure.

In terms of the layout of building ensembles on axes, classical architecture also attained very high competence. Buildings from small residences to huge temples and palaces, with layer upon layer of gardens and courts and innumerable doors and gates, are all arranged in a harmonious and unified layout on one single major axis. In such a composition, contrasting attributes in space, such as high and low, far and near, solid and void, wide and narrow, sparse and dense, are manipulated to yield charmingly varied visual effects. Such accomplished artistry and skill in the handling of axial composition are expressions of the artistic genius of the Chinese people.

One outstanding contribution made by Chinese artisans has been the landscape garden which takes natural scenic beauty as its *leitmotif*. As early as the Eastern Han (first to third century A.D.), there emerged a tradition following the maxim of "Construct the garden according to nature, impound a running stream to form a pond". In the Tang period, the Wangchuan Villa built by the famous poet Wang Wei was enormous in scale and had within it the seclusion afforded by woods and streams, as well as a profusion of bamboo groves and flowers.

Beginning in Tang times, a predilection for rare rocks became the vogue among the literati and this aesthetic was passed on to later generations. The Genyue Hill, which the Song Emperor, Hui Zong, constructed at the capital of Bianjing, was the culmination of the art of building artificial rockery hills in the Song period. After the Yuan and Ming, painters often took part in garden design, bringing to it themes from landscape painting. Ji Cheng of the Ming Dynasty summed up the experience of past generations in his book *Yuan Ye* (*Book on Garden Making*), in which he advocated, even for artificial town gardens, a quality which makes the garden "appear to have grown out of Nature, even though it is an artifact of man". Nature's scenic attributes were to be assembled for man's creative rearrangement. The art of garden-making thus became more theoretically sophisticated, drawing upon the metaphor that classical Chinese gardens were like landscape paintings in the round. This styled garden art is much acclaimed by landscape designers in China and abroad. It is our hope that this kind of landscape painting in three dimensions will break new ground and succeed in reflecting the lifestyles of a new era.

Methodical Management of Building Construction Resulting in Accelerated Building Programs

According to the *Zuo Zhuan*, written during the Warring States Period, methodical management had already been applied during the Spring and Autumn Period in the sixth and fifth century B.C. by the kingdom of Chu. In order to facilitate the construction of a walled city, Chu officials had the building implements readied and the site, earth volumes and hauling distances surveyed. Food and other provisions were assembled; labor and working days were calculated prior to the commencing of actual construction work. With such thorough preparation, the project was completed in just three months. This illustrates the extraordinary emphasis placed on construction management in ancient China.

In terms of organization, a system of construction officers appeared no later than the period of the Warring States. Under this system, which was adopted by succeeding dynasties, the *Jiangzuojian* (Directorate of Public Works) managed the design and construction of royal palaces, temples, mausoleums, bastions and other projects, while water conservancy officers were responsible for hydraulic engineering. The two important publications on the design and construction of classical Chinese architecture — the Song *Yingzao Fashi* (*Treatise on Architectural Methods*) and the *Gongcheng Zuofa Zeli* (*Construction Procedures and Standards*) from Qing Gongbu (Ministry of Works) — were compiled in order to effect more accurate estimates for procurement of labor and materials and to strengthen construction management under the system of official building directorates.

In ancient China, careful consideration was given to the division of work into separate trades. Archaeological excavations have revealed that in the time of the Northern Wei in the fifth century A.D., even the production of earthenware had already been divided into four trades according to the sequence of production: modeling, throwing, cutting and burnishing. In the 11th century, building construction had already been divided into thirteen trades: moats and fortifications, masonry, carpentry, joinery, carving, lathe work, sawing, bamboo-work, tiling, plastering, painting, brick-laying, and kiln-firing. In the 17th century, additions such as earthwork, scaffolding, glazing, sculpting, paper mounting, painting, gilding, and brass-work increased the number of trades to more than thirty.

In building economics, systems of control over material quantities appeared very early. By the 11th century in the Song Dynasty, a set of standards had been established, laying down rational principles for calculations. For instance, to take account of day length variations, summer wages were increased by one tenth and winter wages decreased by the same amount, with a spring or autumn day as the standard working day. In a similar vein, transport charges were determined according to distance, and as to whether the freight traveled downstream with the river's flow or against it upstream. The overall estimates for woodworking were based on how hard or how soft the timber was. In Qing construction regulations, not only was consideration given to working time and material quantities for general types of construction, but calculation procedures and weight standards (e.g. the specification of standard dimensions, weight and volume for the calculation of transport by either men or beasts of burden) were adopted for special categories of work. For example, in the construction of Buddhist statues, all measurements must be given in square *chi* and *cun* (Chinese feet and inches). In the Ministry of Works of the Qing Dynasty an organization called the Suanfang (Quantity Surveyors' Office) had even been set up to deal specially with estimating and measurement.

To achieve methodical management in construction, modular and standardised designs were used as early as the sixth century, while drafting and construction detailing were handled by specialized artisans in the seventh century. The use of standard profiles of structural timber components as design modules for entire buildings in the tenth century made full use of the body of knowledge gained up to that time, and greatly simplified the processing of materials.

Continual improvements in construction management and design increased the speed of construction. In the Tang Dynasty, the reconstruction of Daming Palace, including over ten ceremonial halls, took only a year. In the year 700 A.D., the Sanyang Palace at Songshan Mountain in Henan Province was completed in only three months, using accelerated construction procedures. At the beginning of the Ming Dynasty, the city of Beijing underwent a major reconstruction. The huge project undertaken inside the Forbidden City, including the construction of the stupendous groups of palace buildings and the ancestral temple in front as well as the ten princes' residences totaling eight thousand three hundred and fifty buildings, took only four years to complete.

There is no doubt that in feudal society, speed such as this in erecting buildings of priority relied on the callous exploitation of the peasants through forced conscription and massive mobilization of the labor force. But careful planning and management were also an important factor in ensuring rapid implementation.

Adapting Methods to the Situation; Making Full Use of Materials According to Their Nature

As the major building material in classical Chinese architecture, timber has been in use for several thousand years. Consequently, much expertise and experience in its working and application have accrued. The treatise of *Yingzao Fashi* (*Treatise on Architectural*

15

Methods) states that the proportion of a timber beam in cross section should be 3 to 2, which is indeed the right proportion in order to fashion from round logs the largest possible rectangular timber with a maximum moment of inertia. It also stipulates that such timbers were not to be trimmed down, but should be optimally deployed; if the sectional area of a rectangular timber was not adequate, extra material could be fixed to its top and sides. Carving, however, was not allowed on beam surfaces so as not to undermine the strength of the timber and to ensure structural safety. Tapered structural members such as eave headers and upturned eave rafters were to be formed by diagonal cutting to conserve material. All these rules reflect the notion that "materials are to be fully utilized according to their nature".

As the actual participants, working people knew very well the necessary procedures and the unique characteristics of regional resources and materials. Naturally, the principle of optimal utilization of local material was best exemplified in the buildings of the common people. On the loess plateaus of south Henan and north Shaanxi, pit-dwellings were formed by digging into the amply deep soil stratum. In Turpan, Xinjiang Province, where rain is scare, houses were vaulted over with adobe (sun-dried mud bricks). In the mountain regions of Tibet, bastions were generally built of stone. Rammed-earth walls, as commonly used in all regions, were of course a traditional building technique of ancient origin. In west Fujian, among the extant houses with rammed-earth walls, there are some, as high as three stories, which have endured for more than one hundred years. In the South, the use of local materials to produce bamboo-lattice walls, stone-slab walls, hollow-brick walls, and pebblestone walls was quite common. In certain regions in Yunnan and Guangxi, where the climate is hot and the soil damp, raised dwellings of bamboo framing resting on bamboo stilts were constructed. For roofing, aside from tiles, such local material as thatch, lime-and-earth, reed bundles, slate, etc. have been turned into good use to form numerous regional variants. To meet the needs of a nomadic life, the Mongol and Uygur nationalities constructed round, demountable tents (*zhanbao*) with fur and willow branches. Other fine examples of materials used to good advantage may be cited, such as the 100-meter span Luding Bridge in Sichuan Province which is a suspension bridge constructed of iron chains, and the famous Dujiang Weir (in Guanxian, Sichuan), in the construction of which gabions of woven bamboo containing pebbles were used to bifurcate the water.

In exploring the history and achievements of classical Chinese architecture, one must also notice how the development of architecture has been influenced by cultural and technological interchange among the nationalities of the Chinese people. Responding to their particular needs, these nationalities had, over long periods in history, created individual architectural forms, which preserved superb traditions of their own. Through prolonged contact, they influenced, assimilated, emulated and enriched each other, thereby collectively contributing new and colorful forms to China's architectural heritage.

Also noticeable is the relationship between Chinese classical architecture and that of other countries. Based on the needs of the people in China, alien cultures have been continually and selectively assimilated. For example, Buddhist pagodas and decorative designs are Chinese architectural motifs created through the assimilation and modification of Indian architectural art, which was imported into China as Buddhism spread through the country.

Ancient Chinese architecture, having developed under the fetters of feudalism, inevitably harbors some feudalistic elements and technological constraints. To better preserve and utilize this precious legacy, it is essential, through objective analysis and evaluation, to inherit all of the useful architectural wisdom and experience gained from the past and apply it now to create a new and yet finer architecture.

Chinese Academy of Architecture

June, 1979

The Architecture of Primitive Society
(Circa 600,000 to 4,000 years ago)

Primitive man's dwelling

Beijing   between 400,000 to 500,000 years ago

The internal width of this natural cave on the eastern side of Linggu Hill near Zhoukoudian, Beijing, is 30 meters at its widest point. Large amounts of stone implements, ashes and burnt skeletons discovered inside the cave indicate that Paleolithic man had lived here for a long time and knew the use of fire.

Structural members excavated at Hemudu
Yuyao   Zhejiang   c.5000 B.C.

   With a total area of some 40,000 square meters, the
archaeological site at Hemudu is the earliest Neolithic
building site so far discovered in China. Here, many timber
structural members which bore joints of various kinds have
been excavated. The ability to make such precise and correct
wood joints at a time when stone implements were the only
major tools reflects the grasp ancient Chinese had of
building techniques used in their long struggle against the
elements.

UNIVERSITY
OXFORD
COLLEGE

Archaeological site at Banpo
Xi'an   Shaanxi   c.3600 B.C.

This archaeological site of ancient dwellings was a village belonging to the matriarchal clan society of the Middle Neolithic Period. The total area of about 50,000 square meters was divided into three parts: living quarters, the kiln yards, and communal burial grounds. Surrounded by a moat about five meters deep and six meters wide, the living quarters consisted of forty to fifty closely spaced dwellings of the clan members. In the center stood a large quadrangular building which probably served as the milieu for communal activities such as clan meetings. Individual houses were either quadrangular or circular in plan. The former were mostly of the shallow pit type; the latter were generally built above ground. Doors mostly opened to the south. Inside the house there were gourd-shaped fire pits.

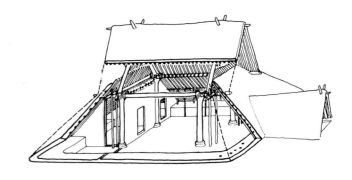

Plan and reconstruction of the quadrangular house

Quadrangular house

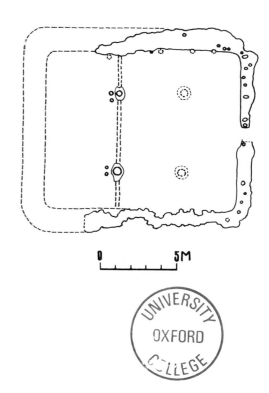

Circular house

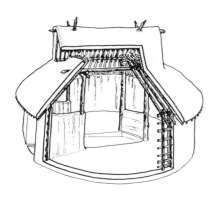

Plan and reconstruction of the circular house

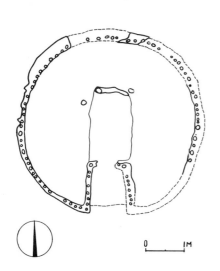

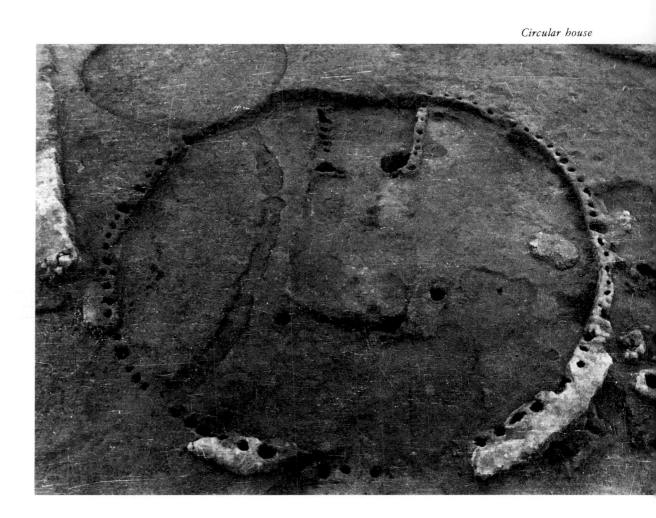

21

Archaeological site at Dahe Village
Zhengzhou   Henan   c.3000 B.C.

 This site belongs to the late Yangshao Cultural Phase of the Neolithic Period. On it was found a house with four connected rooms. There were no interior columns, and the roof was supported on earth walls with wood studs. Onto these studs, horizontal rods were fastened, and then, onto this framework, reed bundles. A mixture of straw and soil plastered on both sides completed the wall construction. The flooring inside was a hard paving of lime and coarse sand. This exemplifies the appearance at that time of multiple-roomed houses, and the use in buildings of small quantities of lime obtained from mortar stone and shells.

The Architecture of
Slave Society

(Circa 2100-476 B.C.)

UNIVERSITY OXFORD COLLEGE

Archaeological site at Erlitou

Yanshi   Henan   Shang Dynasty   c.1590-1300 B.C.

This was the site of a palace of the early Shang period. The buildings stood on a 10,000-square meter terrace of rammed earth which is estimated to be over 20,000 cubic meters in volume. In the middle of the terrace was a eight-bay wide, three-bay deep palace hall. The main gate was on the south side of the terrace, which was surrounded on all four sides by a gallery, forming a complete building ensemble. This is the most ancient palace site so far discovered in China.

Reconstruction

Shang City archaeological site
Zhengzhou   Henan   Shang Dynasty   c.1400 B.C.

Research has revealed this walled city to be Aodu, the capital of the middle Shang. It is roughly square in plan, with a perimeter of 7,100 meters and an area of 320 hectares. The city wall was of rammed earth, battered steeply on the outward side and gently on the inward side, with a base 36 meters wide at its maximum. It is the earliest rammed-earth city wall yet discovered (shown by heavy lines in the figure). Inside the city are sites of Shang houses (in black); outside are numerous archaeological sites (in hatched pattern) including a bronze foundry, brewery, and various workshops for boneware, pottery, etc.

UNIVERSITY OXFORD COLLEGE

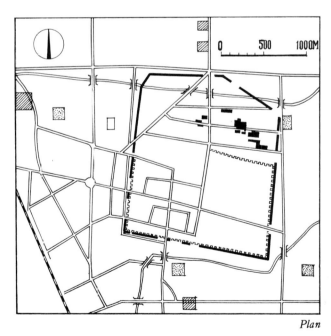

Plan

Archaeological site of Panlong City

Huangpo   Hubei   Shang Dynasty   c.1300 B.C.

Panlong City is the site of an ancient city of the middle Shang period. In its northeast, groups of palace buildings built on a rammed earth terrace have been discovered. The northernmost group had galleries surrounding it on all four sides, with a four room palace hall in the middle measuring 38.2 meters wide and 11 meters deep. Columns supporting the eave purlins had their ends deeply sunken into the base of the hall for stability. The walls were of earth with timber studs.

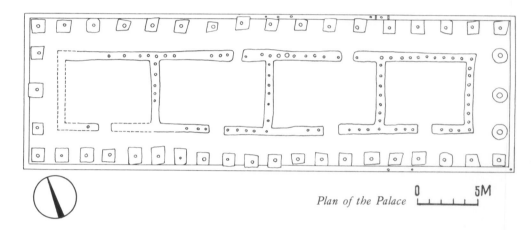

Plan of the Palace   0 ⊢⊢⊢⊢⊣ 5M

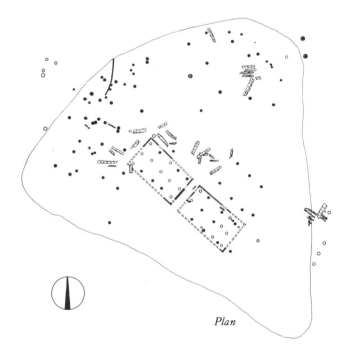

Plan

Archaeological site of Western Zhou buildings

Qichun   Hubei   Western Zhou Dynasty c.1000 B.C.

On this archaeological site of the early Zhou Dynasty were single-storied buildings with columns on the ground floor supporting the floor boards of rooms above. Mortises were carved into the columns to receive beams to which floor boards, approximately two to three centimenters thick were nailed.

Western Zhou roof tiles

Western Zhou   c.1100-771 B.C.

From excavations at Xi'an, Luoyang and other archaeological sites, it is evident that clay tiles had been in use in China as roofing material no later than the end of the Western Zhou Dynasty. They were of various kinds such as segmental tiles, semi-cylindrical tiles, ridge tiles, etc. The segmental tiles shown here were excavated at the archaeological site of the Zhou capital of Fenggao at Kesheng Village, Chang'an, Shaanxi Province, and are of two types, convex and concave, both having eyelets in the back for fastening. Each tile weighs some five kilograms.

Building materials of the Spring and Autumn Period

Spring and Autumn Period 770-476 B.C.

Decorative art on buildings became yet richer and more colorful in the Spring and Autumn Period: on the eave, tile-ends with varied motifs in relief were added to the end of semi-cylindrical tiles; inside, bronze casings covered the connections between timber columns and lintels; tapestries were hung in the interior; furniture had jade, metal and lacquered ornaments on it; floors were covered with standardized bamboo mats.

The tiles and bronze casing shown here are from the excavation at Fengxiang County, Shaanxi Province.

Tile-end with image of doe and fawn

Half-tile ends with images of cloud, deers, birds and tree

Bronze casing

28

The Architecture of Feudal Society
Early Period (475 B.C. to 581 A.D.)

Architectural image in bronze of the Warring States Period

Warring States Period 475-221 B.C.

No above-ground building of the Warring States Period remains, but from the figures on bronzeware, we can note some special features of contemporaneous architecture. For example, there are high raised platforms with many steps, large brackets connected to heads of columns, flat and single-pitched roofs used in combination, floors supported by cross joists, etc. Old records contain descriptions of nobles "building lofty pavilions and pergolas, embellishing palaces" and "vying with each other in opulence". These figures offer tangible illustrations.

Bronze cup and the figure inscribed on its interior surface

Remnants of bronzewares

UNIVERSITY OXFORD COLLEGE

Site of Yan Xiadu

Yixian   Hebei   Warring States Period   4th-3rd century B.C.

Xiadu of the State of Yan, 8,300 meters long from east to west, and 4,000 meters wide from north to south, consisted of an inner and outer city. In the inner city a series of building sites, such as the Wuyang Terrace and Laomu Terrace, have been found. The outer city to the west was the handicrafts zone where iron and bronze foundries, kilns and other workshops were located. Royal tombs occupied another zone to the northwest.

Large quantities of semi-cylindrical tiles, segmental tiles and semi-circular tile-ends have been excavated from this archaeological site. The largest semi-cylindrical tiles are as long as 71 centimeters. Tile-ends and the backs of some of the semi-cylindrical tiles bear moulded patterns of intricate design, and some tile surfaces were polished and painted vermilion. In addition, drainage pipes, circular or pentagonal in section, and gargoyles of an animal head design have also been discovered.

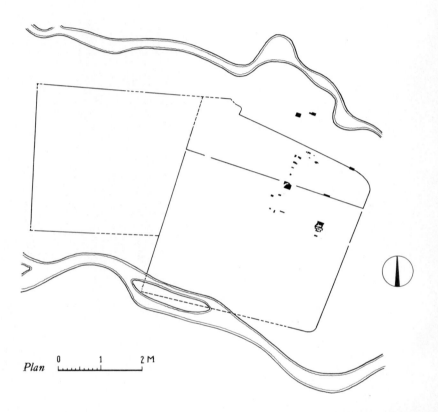

Plan   0   1   2 M

Laomu Terrace

West wall of the outer city

Semi-cylindrical tile

Gargoyle with an animal head design

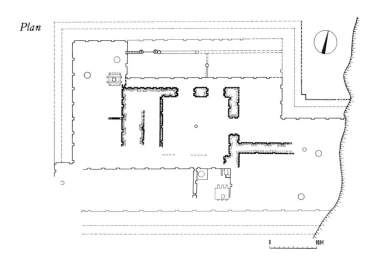

Plan

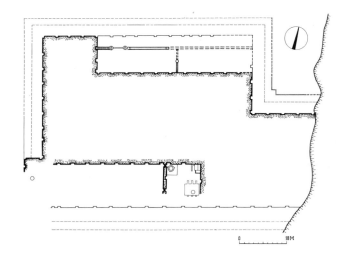

Archaeological site of Xianyang Palace, State of Qin

Xianyang   Shaanxi   Warring States Period   350-207 B.C.

In his effort to reform, Emperor Xiao of the state of Qin moved the capital to Xianyang, and had extensive palaces built there. The illustration shows the site where one of these major palaces once stood. It is a six-meter high rammed-earth podium, measuring 45 meters wide from north to south, and 60 meters long from east to west. The palace compartments were spaced on top of this earth podium and around its perimeter, forming a great palace of rising tiers, as was typical of buildings on high podia in vogue at the time of the Warring States. Floors were painted scarlet red, and colorful murals were painted on the inner walls. Some of the rooms had fireplaces in the walls for heating and also had storm water sumps. Seven storage cellars served the whole palace complex. All these reflect the high standards of architectural design at that time.

Panorama

Foundation of the palace on the podium

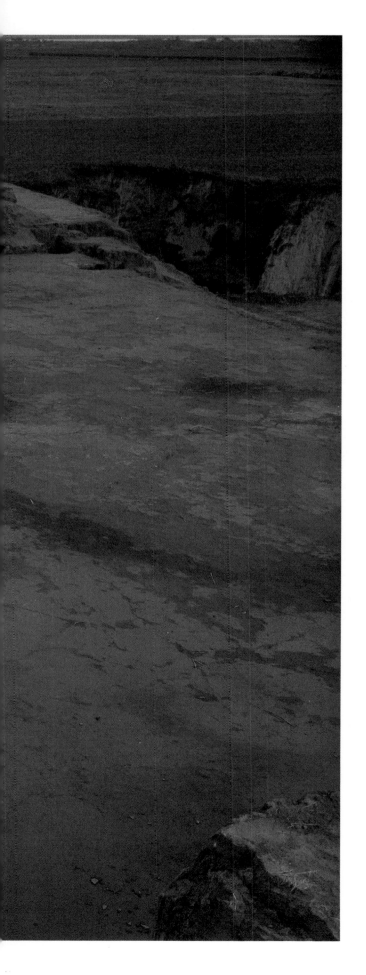

Wall facing brick

UNIVERSITY OXFORD COLLEGE

Hollow brick steps

Dujiang Weir

Guanxian   Sichuan   Warring States Period   250 B.C.

Dujiang Weir was built under the direction of Li Bing, governor of Shu Prefecture (present-day Sichuan) at the time of Emperor Zhao of Qin. To facilitate the flow of water, a bifurcation dyke was constructed at the center of the Min River, the water of which was hence divided into an inner and outer stream. The inner stream, routed past Baopingkou, irrigates the plains of Guanxian. Superfluous water flows back to join the outer stream via a spillway dam. A stone figure, erected on one of the banks, serves as water level gauage. "Dredge wherever it is deep, dyke wherever it is shallow". Derived from experience, this has been adhered to as the principal rule of maintenance. After over two thousand years of constant use and improvements, Dujiang Weir plays an important role in flood prevention, irrigation, and transportation to this day.

Ling Canal

Xing'an Guangxi Qin Dynasty 214 B.C.

After unifying China, the First Emperor of Qin had the Ling Canal (Lingqu) constructed by excavating at the lowest point of the watershed between the Xiang River and the Li River. Linking the two great river systems of the Yangtze River and the Pearl River, the Ling Canal is navigable and provides water for irrigation, and has served to enhance the north-south economic development of China. Among the extant works of hydraulic engineering, the interesting features of the present-day Ling Canal are the shearwater ends, the spillway dams of Datianping and Xiaotianping, and the chutes which maintain a balance of the water levels.

UNIVERSITY OXFORD COLLEGE

Xiaotianping Spillway Dam

Mausoleum of the First Emperor of Qin

Lintong Shaanxi Qin Dynasty 210 B.C.

Yingzheng, the First Emperor of Qin, was a famous statesman of ancient China who established the first centralised, multi-racial feudal Chinese empire. By his order, several hundred thousand workers were deployed to build this colossal mausoleum.

The mausoleum consists of an earth mound in the center with an inner and an outer enclosure. The earth mound itself is 76 meters high, 485 meters wide and 515 meters long at the base. The perimeter of the inner enclosure is 2,525.4 meters while that of the outer enclosure is 6,294 meters. Relics of architectural interest abound in the vicinity. Among those that have been unearthed are door pivot blocks, column bases, ridge tiles, tile-ends, stone conduits, clay conduits, and bronze structural members. They reflect some of the achievements of building art in the Qin period.

Bronze structural members

Tile-end

Pentagonal clay conduit

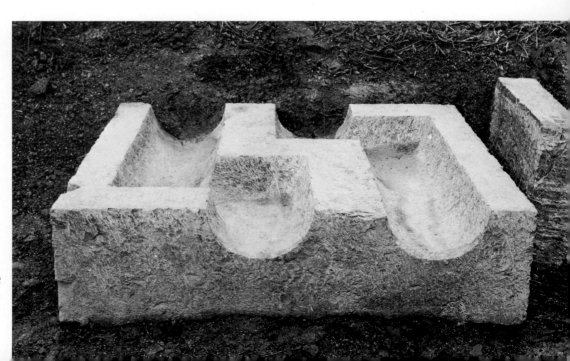

Stone conduit

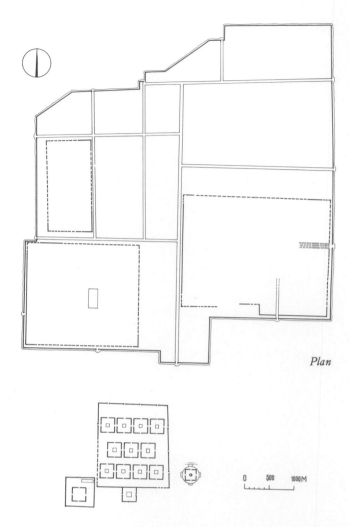

Plan

Historic site of Han Chang'an

Xi'an   Shaanxi   Western Han   206 B.C. - 23 A.D.

This historic site is situated to the northwest of Xi'an. The perimeter of the rammed-earth city wall, remnants of which still remain, measures 25.1 kilometers, punctuated by twelve city gates. In the center and in the southern part of the city were located palaces and government offices, the former including several huge palaces such as the Weiyang Palace and Changluo Palace. In the northeast part were situated government handicraft workshops, while the northeast corner was where the inhabitants concentrated. At the time of Emperor Wu of Han, the Kunming Lake was excavated to serve as an important source of water supply for the capital. The immense Jianzhang Palace was also built. Towards the end of the Western Han, when Wang Mang took over the government, ritual buildings such as ancestral temples were built at the southern part of the city.

Ruins of a ritual building

Ruins of Xuanping Gate

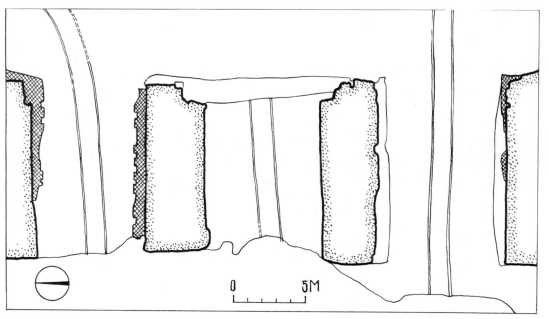

Plan of Xuanping Gate

Han bricks and tiles

Han Dynasty   206-220 A.D.

Bricks and tiles were used to a far greater extent in the Han than in the Warring States Period, as evidenced by the large number of Han bricks, tiles and other materials that have been excavated. Vaulting had already been commonly used in brick tombs. There were also various standardized brick types such as wedge bricks and fan-shaped bricks for arch construction, large-sized bricks with tongue-and-grooved edges for jointing, as well as columnar and hollow tiles.

Han tile-ends are all circular, with characters, icons of animals, plants and other patterns as ornament. Sometimes the location for the tile's use is indicated by the ornamentation. For instance, qinglong *(green dragon)* represents east; baihu *(white tiger)*, west; zhuque *(scarlet bird)*, south; and xuanwu *(tortoise and snake)*, north.

Tile-end with image of green dragon (Qinglong)

Tile-end with image of scarlet bird (zhuque)

Tile-end with image of white tiger (baihu)

Tile-end with image of tortoise and snake (xuanwu)

UNIVERSITY
OXFORD
COLLEGE

Wedge-shaped tiles with tongue-and-grooved joints

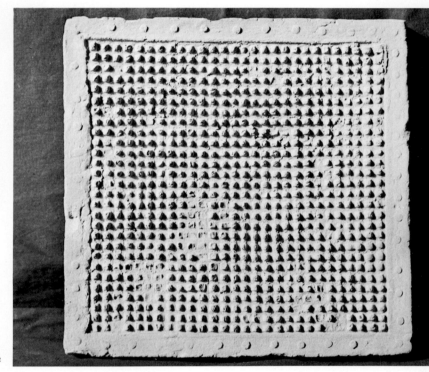

Paving tile with studded design

Hollow brick with image of two phoenixes

43

Green glazed burial article, Western Han

Colored burial article, Eastern Han

44

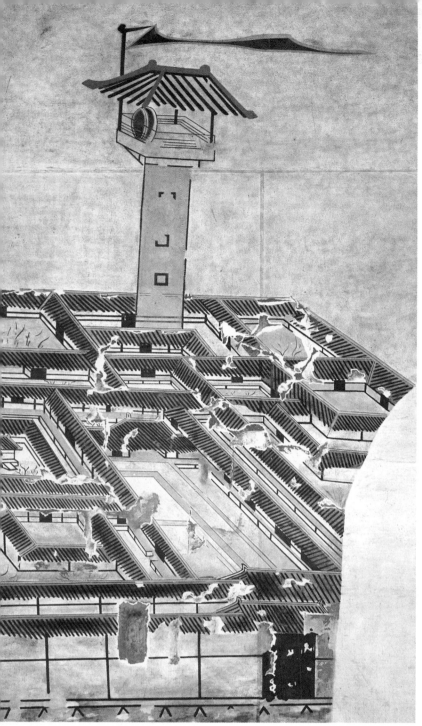

Mural in a Han tomb in Anping, Hebei

UNIVERSITY OXFORD COLLEGE

Green glazed burial article, Eastern Han

Burial articles, murals and bricks with moulded designs in Han tombs of architectural interest
Han Dynasty 206-220 B.C.

A considerable number of burial articles, murals, bricks with moulded designs and tomb-in-cliff carvings have been unearthed from excavated Han tombs. Examples are the various clay houses discovered in Guangzhou, clay towers dug up in Henan and Hebei, and clay fortresses unearthed in Guangzhou and Gansu. Also there are the painted clay houses and courts of landlords depicted on murals in the Han tomb at Anping, Hebei; the city layouts represented on the murals in the Han tombs in Horinger, Inner Mongolia; as well as the images of residences and bridges stamped or carved on brick or stone that have been unearthed in various other places. These materials illustrate the resourceful forms and the gigantic scale of Han architecture.

Han brick with moulded design discovered at Chengdu

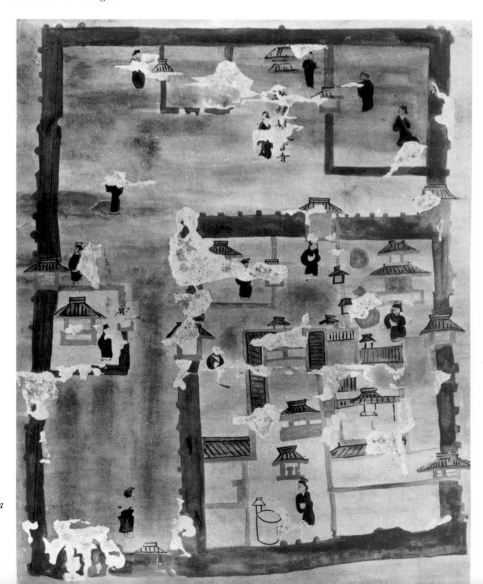

Mural in Horinger, Inner Mongolia

Han watchtowers

Eastern Han   25-220 A.D.

Stone watchtowers in front of large Han tombs signify entrances to the tomb compounds. Structural details on the podium, corbel brackets, eaves, etc. are carefully carved, based on timber watchtower designs. A good number of Han stone watchtowers of various types are extant in Sichuan, Henan, Shantong and other places. The picture shows the Jun Watchtower built during the Eastern Han between 190-193. A.D. at Pingyang Fu, Mianyang County, Sichuan Province.

Jun Watchtower at Pingyang Fu

Grottoes of the Northern Dynasties
Northern and Southern Dynasties 5-6th century A.D.

During the Northern and Southern Dynasties the feudal rulers, in their patronage of Buddhism, had a large number of grotto shrines constructed in northern China by excavation. These shrines were usually cut out of steep precipices on a stupendous scale. Exquisitely carved and sculpted, the grotto shrines have preserved a great number of sculptures of high aesthetic value, among which are many revealing images of architectural forms from that time. Such grottoes as the thirtieth cave and the Seven Buddha Pavilion of Maiji Mountain, the sixteenth cave of Tianlong Mountain, the galleries along the fifth and sixth caves of Beixiangtang Mountain, the coffered ceiling of the fourth cave at Gongxian, the second and tenth caves and the central column of West Pagoda Cave at Yungang, together with their many bas-reliefs of pagodas, halls, gateways, and galleries, offer researchers information on the architecture of the Northern and Southern Dynasties.

Exterior view of the Tenth Cave at Yungang

UNIVERSITY
OXFORD
COLLEGE

*Front gallery of the Tenth
Cave at Yungang*

Relief in Guyang Cave at
Longmen

Exterior view of the Sixteenth Cave at Tianlong Mountain

Ceiling of the Fourth Cave at Gongxian, Henan

Panorama of Maiji Mountain

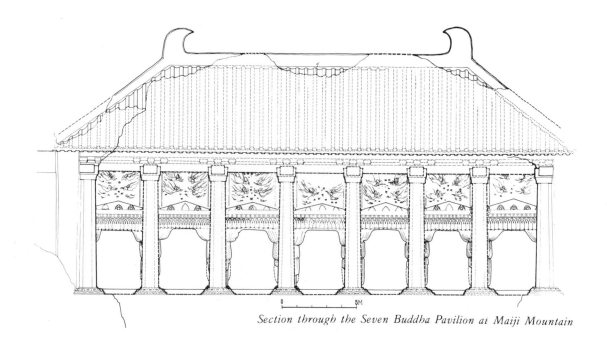

Section through the Seven Buddha Pavilion at Maiji Mountain

Stone Carving at the Tomb of Xiao Ji

Gourong   Jingsu   Northern and Southern Dynasties   529 A.D.

Guardian beasts, unicorns, grave avenue columns, steles and other carvings were installed in front of the mausoleums of the Southern Dynasties (420-589 A.D.) which were situated around Nanjing, Jiangling, Danyang, Gourong and other places in Jiangsu Province. The tomb of Xiao Ji of the Liang Dynasty (502-557 A.D.) is a relatively well preserved example. These stone guardian beasts are especially powerful looking, revealing an extremely high level of artistry. Each stone beast was carved out of one single rock more than 30 cubic meters in volume.

Guardian beast

UNIVERSITY
OXFORD
COLLEGE

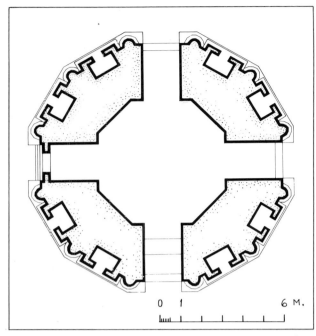

Pagoda of Songyue Monastery

Dengfeng   Henan   Northern and Southern Dynasties   523 A.D.

Songyue Monastery is a famous example from the
Northern Wei Period. Of all the existing buildings there,
this pagoda is the only authentic original. It is also the
earliest intact brick building in ancient Chinese architecture.
It consists basically of a cylinder, hollow from top to bottom,
with an outer diameter of 10.7 meters and an inner
diameter of 5.9 meters at the base. The bricks, laid in clay
mortar, follow a gentle parabolic profile that is precise and
balanced, demonstrating fully the high degree of construction
skills of the Chinese working people as far back as one
thousand four hundred years ago.

0   1   6 M.

Plan

Yi Ciwei Stone Memorial Column

Yixian Hebei Northern and Southern Dynasties 567-570 A.D.

Standing at a cemetry, this seven-meter high stone memorial column is the only actual example so far discovered of ancient memorial pillars. It resembles the huabiao pillar (carved ornamented pillars standing, usually in pairs, before the gates of palaces and tombs) somewhat in form, but has an extra large top on which three small halls were precisely carved.

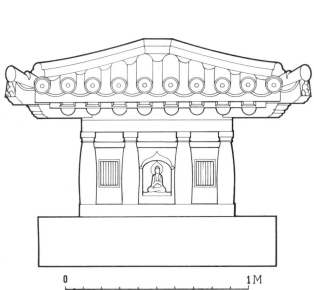

0   1 M

Section of the small hall on top of the memorial column

The Architecture of
Feudal Society

Middle Period (581-1368 A.D.)

Four Entrance Pagoda of Shentong Temple

Licheng   Shandong   Sui Dynasty   611 A.D.

   Constructed entirely with laid stones, this is the earliest stone pagoda extant in China. The pagoda is square in plan, single-storied, with entrances on all four sides and layered eaves. This type of pagoda is shown in grotto carvings or on murals of the Northern and Southern Dynasties, and is one of the common pagoda types of the early Buddhist period.

Earthen House of the Sui Dynasty

Sui Dynasty   581-618 A.D.

Fairly complete contemporary architectural details are represented in this earthen house. The hooked lateral ridge, the vertical ridge butted with tiles in the shape of animals, the column head bracket set with four simplified outward corbelling layers, octagonal eave-columns, tied lotus decoration in the mid-parts of the columns, inverted-lotus type column bases, and ground tie-beams all illustrate accurately the exterior forms and structural characteristics of contemporaneous architecture.

UNIVERSITY OXFORD COLLEGE

Anji Bridge

Zhaoxian Hebei Sui Dynasty 589-608 A.D.

Also known as Zhaozhou Bridge or Dashi Bridge, this was constructed under the direction of the famous engineer Li Chun of the Sui Dynasty. It is a large-span, single-arch bridge with open spandrels. The supporting arch has a clear span of 37.37 meters, and is made up of twenty-eight 34-cm wide arches laid side by side. On either side of this supporting arch, two smaller arches perforate the spandrel above the main arch, thereby reducing the dead-weight of the spandrels, increasing the stability of the main arch, allowing flood water to pass through, and facilitating maintenance. It is the earliest open-spandrel stone arch bridge in the world.

Close-up view

Carvings on the balustrades

Rubbing of a Song carving of Tang Chang'an

Historic site of Sui and Tang Chang'an
Xi'an Shaanxi Sui Dynasty · 582 A.D.

In the second year of the reign of Emperor Wen of the Sui Dynasty, the city of Daxing, which was renamed Chang'an in the Tang Dynasty, was built to the southeast of the Han city of Chang'an. With an outer city wall measuring 9,721 meters from east to west and 8,651.7 meters from north to south, Chang'an was the largest city in ancient China. The palace compound and the royal residence compound were situated in the center of the north side of the city. In the front, the 155-meter wide Boulevard of Zhuquemen, with three-meter wide drainage ditches on either side, ran straight to the Mingde Gate, the southern gate of the city. The city was divided into one hundred and ten fang (residential neighborhoods) and two shi (marketplaces).

In Tang times, the Daming Palace was built on high ground in the northern section, overlooking the entire city. In the three-hectare palace compound, over thirty sites of palace halls have already been excavated, including such large examples as Hanyuan Hall and Linde Hall.

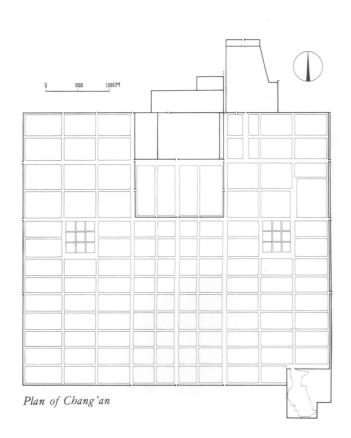

Plan of Chang'an

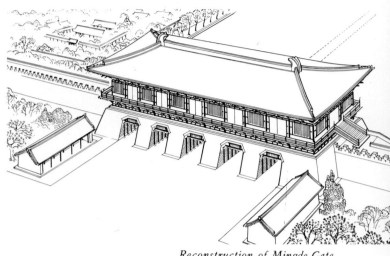

Reconstruction of Mingde Gate

Site of Mingde Gate

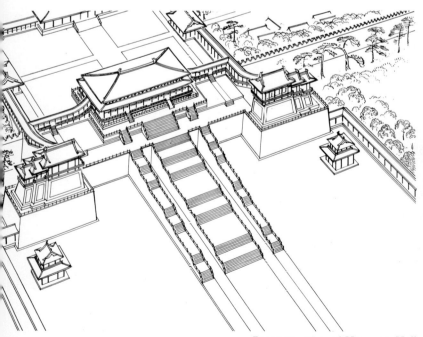

Site of Hanyuan Hall of Daming Palace

Reconstruction of Hanyuan Hall

Dayan Pagoda of Ci'en Monastery

Xi'an Shaanxi Tang Dynasty 704 A.D.

This 64-meter high pagoda is of brick wall and wood floor construction. The top floor affords a bird's-eye view of the whole of Chang'an City, including Qujiang Lake. The pagoda was a popular sight-seeing spot at that time. A layer of bricks was laid surrounding the pagoda in the Ming Dynasty when it was refurbished and strengthened. Engraved on the four lintels at the ground floor of the pagoda were pictures, among which one depicts a five-bayed Buddhist temple hall in which the style and characteristics of timber construction in the early Tang are revealed.

Mural in the Tomb of Prince Yide

Qianxin   Shaanxi   Tang Dynasty   705-706 A.D.

The tomb of Li Chongrun, Prince Yide, is adjacent to the imperial mausoleum of Qian Ling. Excavated in 1971, this underground tomb consists of an access passage, a paved path, and two coffin chambers, one in the front and the other at the rear. The total length is 100.8 meters. All walls enclosing the tomb passage and the chambers are lined with painted murals. One section of the murals depicts a gate tower. Also depicted in the mural is a brick podium which is paved along the margin of its steps and at its four corners with slabs of elaborately carved stone. On the podium rises a dais which in turn supports three gate towers with wudian style roofs (hipped roofs) and two secondary gate towers in the same style. The construction details shown on this mural closely resemble those depicted on the stone carving on the lintel of the Dayan Pagoda.

UNIVERSITY OXFORD COLLEGE

Xiaoyan Pagoda of Jianfu Monastery

Xi'an Shaanxi Tang Dynasty 707-709 A.D.

This is a Tang masterpiece with a square-shaped plan, a hollow central shaft and tiers of solid decorative eaves on its exterior. It is 40 odd meters high, while the ground floor measures 11.25 meters on each side of the square plan. In the base are buried timber grillages to increase the integrity of the foundation. Although it has experienced three severe earthquakes and there are cracks on the walls, it did not collapse. After the establishment of the People's Republic, it was repaired and strengthened.

UNIVERSITY OXFORD COLLEGE

Main Hall of Nanchan Monastery
Wutai   Shanxi   Tang Dynasty   782 A.D.
  In plan the main hall is 11.62 meters wide and 9.67 meters long. It is the earliest timber structure extant in China. To better preserve this building, thorough repairs were made in 1974.

Interior view of the main hall of Nanchan Monastery

Front eave

East Hall of Foguang Temple

Wutai Shanxi Tang Dynasty 857 A.D.

Foguang Temple was one of the most famous Buddhist temples in Wutai Mountain during the Tang Dynasty. Its east hall is divided into seven bays widthwise totaling 34 meters, and eight portions lengthwise totaling 17.66 meters. The roof is in the wudian style (hipped), with a single layer eave. Columns inside and outside of the hall are of the same length. These columns, together with the architrave girders, corbel brackets and tie beams, form a strong structure which remains intact after more than one thousand and one hundred years. The corbel bracket and tie beams together make a good artistic design. Perserved in this typical hall architecture of timber structure are inscriptions, murals and more than thirty statues which are all precious artifacts of the Tang Dynasty.

Distant view

67

UNIVERSITY OXFORD COLLEGE

Front eave

69

Close-up view of Mingci Pavilion in Foguang Temple

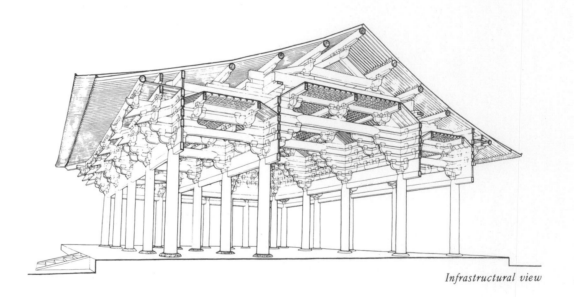

Infrastructural view

Interior view

Stone lantern

Ning'an   Heilongjiang   Tang Dynasty   7-8th century A.D.

The six-meter high stone lantern stands on the site of the First Monastery in Longquan Fu of the ancient Beihai District. In most of the Tang monasteries this sort of lantern was used to line both sides of the walkway in the courtyard. There are very few in existence now and this is the tallest one left.

Ruins of Gaochang City

Ruins of Tang City

Xinjiang   Tang Dynasty   7-10th century A.D.

The central government exercised control over the Xinjiang district as far back as the Han Dynasty. These pictures show Gaochang City and Jiaohe City (near present-day Turpan), both of which were very prosperous during the Tang Dynasty. In some respects the planning of the residential districts in these cities is similar to the lifang structure (with all neighboring residential units square in plan) of the Tang inland cities. Great numbers of Tang official and private documents and fabrics have been found around the ruins, illustrating the long existence of cultural exchange between the nationalities.

Ruins of Jiaohe City

UNIVERSITY OXFORD COLLEGE

Qianxun Pagoda of Chongsheng Temple

Dali   Yunnan   Tang Dynasty
8th century A.D.

Built in the most prosperous period of Nan Zhao, this pagoda is some 60 meters high. Nan Zhao was inhabited by minority nationalities in ancient times, and was located a few thousand li (one Tang li is about 540 meters) southwest of the capital of Chang'an. Transportation was extremely difficult. The form of this pagoda is identical to those in Guanzhong district where the square plan and solid decorative eaves were very popular. This shows that both culture and technique were frequently exchanged among the nationalities.

Dagoba in Qixia Temple
Nanjing Jiangsu Five Dynasties
937-975 A.D.

This dagoba is about 15 meters
high and completely built of stone
which is beautifully carved. On
the xumi style base were carved
not only the story of the Buddha
but also architectural forms of the
Five Dynasties Period.

UNIVERSITY OXFORD COLLEGE

Twin Pagodas of Lingyin Temple
Hangzhou   Zhejiang   Northern Song Dynasty
960 A.D.

*   The twin pagodas of Lingyin Temple are
built entirely of stone and possess finely
carved doors, windows, columns, brackets
and other construction details.*

Yunyan Pagoda
Jiangsu Suzhou Five Dynasties 959 A.D.

Yunyan Pagoda, also known as Huqiu Pagoda, is entirely built of bricks arranged in two walls. Between the inner and the outer walls is the corridor; within the inner wall is the central chamber. This sort of construction did not only divide the space according to function, but also increased the stability of the structure. Building of the inner structure in brick was quite advanced between the late Tang and early Song.

Painting of a hydraulic mill

Five Dynasties   907-960 A.D.

   This picture is believed to be the work of Wei Xian, a famous painter of the Five Dynasties Period. The main subject of the picture is a hydraulic mill, with detailed depiction of the architecture as well as the installation of the mill. It provides an important information reference for the industrial architecture of the Five Dynasties and early Song.

Longhua Pagoda

Shanghai   Northern Song Dynasty   977 A.D.

With cantilever eaves bending elegantly upward, the pagoda is built of brick and its perimeter galleries of timber. The structure has been popular since the Song. After 1949 timber piles of 14 × 18 cm were discovered under the foundation. These are the earliest known piles in China.

UNIVERSITY OXFORD COLLEGE

Twin Pagodas of Lohan Temple

Suzhou   Jiangsu   Northern Song Dynasty 982 A.D.

These twin pagodas are identical in their octagonal plans. The buildings are seven stories high, open inside, with timber floor boards. Each floor has external openings on every other side of the octagon and these openings are in turn rotated 45° at every floor in order to distribute the loading evenly, thus avoiding any cracking of the walls below the openings.

79

Dule Monastery

Tianjin Jixin Liao Dynasty 984 A.D.

Among the Dule Monastery buildings, the main gate and the Hall of Guanyin date from the Liao Dynasty, built in the second year of the Tong He reign. Measuring 20.23 meters in width and 22.5 meters in height, the construction of the Hall of Guanyin is similar to the Foguan Temple of the Tang Dynasty. Making use of a timber structure, this hall has a vertical central space housing the 16-meter high Guanyin (Avalokiteśvara) statue. Dule Monastery has survived twenty-eight earthquakes, including the one in 1679 in the Ping Valley and San River district, which reached the eighth point when "no official buildings and folk dwellings were left standing except the Hall of Guanyin". After the 1976 Tangshan earthquake the hall remained standing, demonstrating once more its stable and sound construction.

Main gate

Guanyin Hall

Corbel brackets of the outer eaves, Guanyin Hall

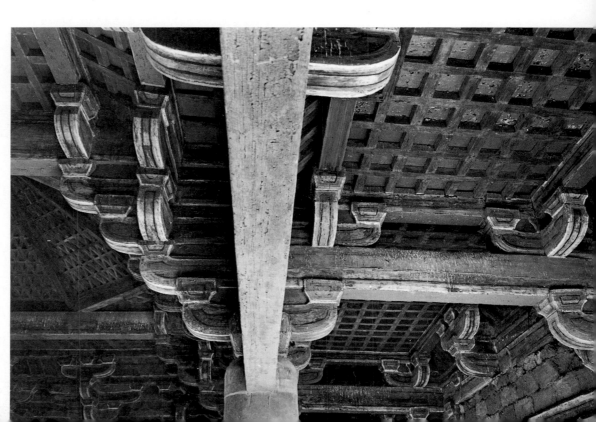

Corbel brackets of the inner eaves, Guanyin Hall

Interior view of
Guanyin Hall

82

UNIVERSITY OXFORD COLLEGE

Main Hall of Baoguo Monastery

Ningbo   Zhejiang   Northern Song   11th century

The main hall of this monastery has a width of 11.91 meters, divided into three bays, and a length of 13.35 meters, again divided into three bays. The roof is of the xieshan *type, single eaved. During the Qing Dynasty a bay was added on each side of the main hall, making a fine building composition with five bays and double layered eaves. The main hall is simple in construction, reflecting the native building methods south of the Yangtze River in the Song. Inside the main hall the earliest examples in China of the reverse fluted timber column and pitched, octagonal ceiling can be seen.

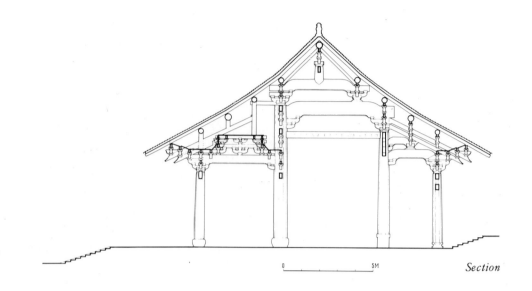

Section

Overall view

Detail of structure

Interior view

Sanqing Hall of Xuanmiao Taoist Temple

Putian   Fujian   Northern Song   1016 A.D.

Although this temple was restored twice during the late
Ming Dynasty, it retains the construction techniques of the
Northern Song: the roof frame in the three bays at the
center is constructed with down pointing cantilever brackets
(Xia'ang) which are connected to lateral beams.

Interior view

85

Interior view

Main Hall of Fengguo Temple

Yixian Liaoning Liao Dynasty 1020 A.D.

The hall is grand in scale, having a width of 48.2 meters divided into nine bays, and a height of 21 meters. It is covered with a hipped roof, single eaved. In cross section, the roof is supported by timber columns varying in height according to the pitch, with the cross-beams of the short columns tenoned into the tall ones, forming a system of cross frames. In longitudinal section, architrave girders, lateral beams, purlins and other components are joined together into a distinctive type of structure. Inside the hall the original five-color Liao paintings abound and the colorful Flying Gandharvas have been preserved.

Outside view

Shengmu Hall of Jin Ancestral Temple

Taiyuan Shanxi Northern Song Dynasty 1023-1031 A.D.

The Jin Ancestral Temple is situated at the foot of Mount Xuanweng, 50 li southwest of Taiyuan. The Shengmu Hall is one of the main buildings. The "columns" supporting the upper eaves do not reach the floor but rather rest on beams spanning between an inner and an outer row of columns. The external wall and fenestration are set back to the plane of the inner row of columns, thus creating a spacious portico in front. Inside the hall there are 43 Song statues which are sculptural masterpieces. In front of the hall there is a cross four-way bridge over a fish pond. The construction reveals much of the Song style.

UNIVERSITY OXFORD COLLEGE

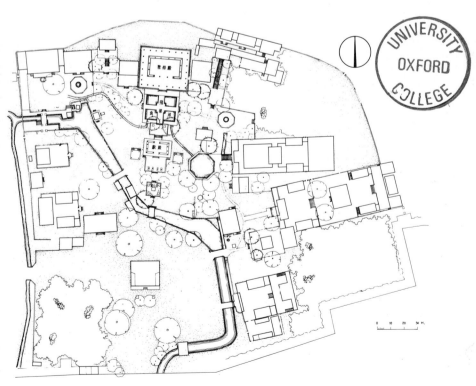

Plan of Jin Ancestral Temple

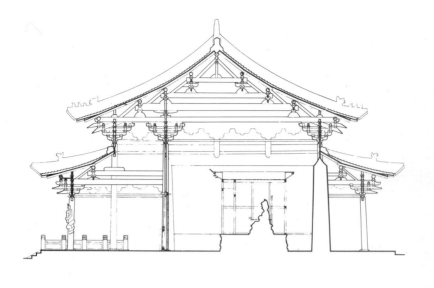

Section

Front eave

Library for Bhagavad Sūtras of Xiahuayan Monastery

Datong   Shanxi   Liao Dynasty   1038 A.D.

This library occupied a whole hall. On the four walls are wooden wall-recessed scripture cabinets in the form of pavilions. The cabinets are divided into two parts, the lower part for scriptures and the upper for a recessed ciboria. The base, balustrades, brackets and roof are all made in strict proportion. They are in fact excellent architectural models as well as outstanding handicraft pieces. The 32 statues inside the hall are original Liao pieces.

UNIVERSITY OXFORD COLLEGE

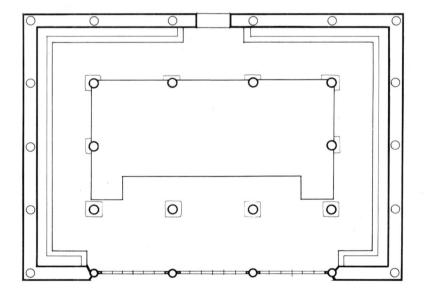

5   0   10 M

Plan

*Cabinets of the
western wall*

Arch bridge in the middle of a cabinet

91

Pagoda of Kaiyuan Temple
Dingxian   Hebei   Northern Song Dynasty
1001-1055 A.D.

This pagoda is also called the
Liaodi Pagoda. With a height of
84 meters it is the highest ancient
pagoda built in brick. From the
first floor upwards the corbelled
eaves serve as balconies as well as
canopies. This technique is
peculiar to the Song. Inside the
pagoda various graphic patterns are
carved on the ceilings of the
corridors, exhibiting the excellence
of ancient brick carving.

Pagoda of Youguo Temple
Kaifeng Henan Northern Song
1044 A.D.

This pagoda is entirely built of brick and has a diameter of 10.24 meters at the base and a height of 57.34 meters. Both inside and outside iron-colored glazed bricks are used. Because of this, it is also called the Iron Pagoda, and is the oldest glazed brick pagoda in existence. The glazed decorative veneer is made up of various small pre-fired units of regular shapes. These units, complicated in shape and numerous in kind, exquisite and accurate in design and workmanship, are used for eave, gallery and bracket as well as door and window details.

Śākyamuni Pagoda of Fogong Temple

Yingxian Shanxi Liao Dynasty 1056 A.D.

The entire pagoda is constructed in wood; hence, it is also called the Wooden Pagoda of Yingxian. The diameter at the base is 30.27 meters with a height of 67.31 meters while the timber portion rises 51.14 meters. It is the oldest surviving timber pagoda of China and the tallest timber building in the world. A series of column brackets and beams form one whole pagoda structure which consists of ten structural tiers: five colonnaded floors, four perimeter galleries each supported by its concealed structural loft, and the top roof structure. Stability is achieved through the superimposition of one tier upon another, each being in itself a structural entity.

UNIVERSITY OXFORD COLLEGE

Detail

95

Interior view

Interior view showing structural loft at the fourth level

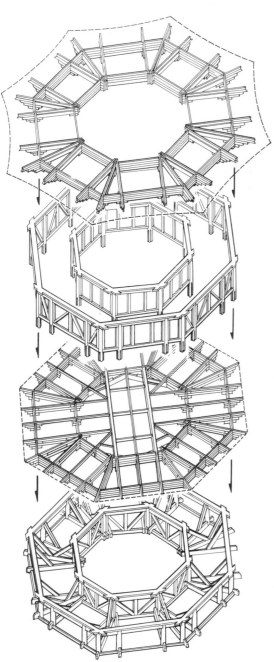

Graphic illustration of structures

0   5   10M

Section

Ten Thousand Avataṃsake Sūtra Pagoda

Hohhot Inner Mongolia Liao Dynasty 916-1125 A.D.

Commonly known as the White Pagoda, it is situated in the Liao city of Feng Zhou and is entirely built of brick and painted white. It was repaired during the Jin Dynasty (1115-1234). On the top floor it has a domed ceiling over a clear space which enjoys a commanding view.

Luoyang Bridge
Hui'an   Fujian   Northern Song Dynasty   1053 A.D.

   Measuring 834 meters long and 7 meters wide, this bridge has 46 piers. To lay the foundation in the deep water and strong current, a huge amount of rocks were dumped across the river. A homgeneous foundation for the piers was formed by the hard oyster shells which grew with cementing effect in the crevices between the rocks. Piers were then built on top. This is the earliest form of raft foundation in China.

Mulan Dyke
Putian   Fujian   Northern Song Dynasty   1075 A.D.

   Mulan Dyke was an irrigation engineering effort carried out by the farmers in Northern Song. This water barrier lies across the Mulan River at Putian just before it runs into the sea and manages to separate the fresh water of the river running down stream from the rising tides of salt sea water. A total of 160,000 mu (1 mu equals 0.0667 hectares) of rice field is thus irrigated. There are still 126 meters of the dyke with 28 gate outlets in existence. The dyke is of stone construction with a base width of 80 meters and height of over ten meters. Up to this day the construction remains very firm and stable.

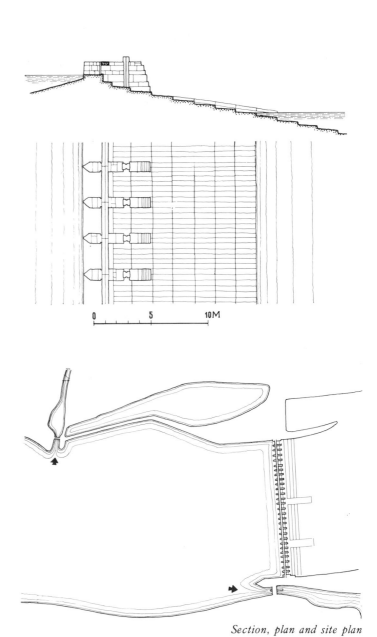

Section, plan and site plan

River Scene During Ching Ming Festival

Northern Song Dynasty   c.1125 A.D.

"River Scene During Ching Ming Festival" was painted by Zhang Zeduan towards the end of the Northern Song Dynasty (960-1127), depicting the townsfolk leaving the capital for the countryside. This long scroll therefore includes some urban architectural scenes of the time, such as the city gate, bridges, shops, tea houses, residential houses, etc. They provide important information for the study of Song architecture. This reproduction is part of the scroll showing a segment of the Rainbow Bridge which was constructed by strutting short pieces of timber together to span the river without the support of columns. It was an intricate construction method.

Jinming Pool
Southern Song Dynasty   post 1127 A.D.

Jinming Pool was a palace garden in the west of the capital city Bianliang during the Northern Song Dynasty. Recorded to have a circumference of nine li and thirty bu (about 5070 meters), the pool used to be the racing ground for dragon-boats and various water acrobatics during the third lunar month every year. The picture here, drawn by a Southern Song artist, depicts the layout of the garden and the building.

Coffered ceiling in the hall of Jingtu Temple

Yingxian   Shanxi   Jin Dynasty   1124 A.D.

   The ceiling of the main hall is made up of recessed square, hexagonal and octagonal coffers, surrounded by ornaments of the "celestial pavilion" type. These ornaments are beautifully carved in proportion, exemplying the level of decorative joinery in the Jin Dynasty.

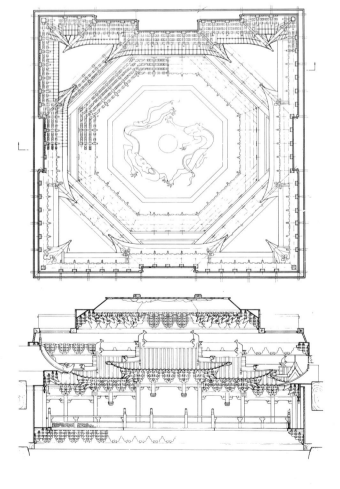

Plane and section

Zhuanlunzang Hall

Longxing Temple

Zhengding Hebei Northern Song and Jin dynasties 960-1234 A.D.

Built in the Song Dynasty, the temple retains its original layout. The main building, Muni (Śakyamuni) Hall, was erected in 1052, with its roof in the xieshan *(half-hipped, half-gabled)* style and double eaved. Projecting from each of the four sides of the main structure is an ancillary hall with its top rising like a "tortoise head". Such a style of building is commonly depicted in ancient paintings, but the Longxing Temple is the only actual example. Besides the Muni Hall, there are also the Cishe Pavilion and Zhuanlunzang Hall. Though repaired many times, they are still basically Song architecture. Their exterior forms are the same, but their interior trabeations are of different construction in response to different functional requirements.

Muni Hall

Coffered ceiling of the third floor corridor

Pagoda of Bao'en Temple

Suzhou   Jiangsu   Southern Song Dynasty   1131-1162 A.D.

An octagonal, nine-story brick pagoda, its base, wooden eaves, basement and secondary stairs were repaired in later periods and are not original works of the Southern Song. The body of the pagoda is made up of walls and an inner structure, with small chambers in the latter. The brick beams, architrave girders, brackets, octagonal ceiling coffers and the top floor column all retain the appearance of timber construction of the Song.

UNIVERSITY OXFORD COLLEGE

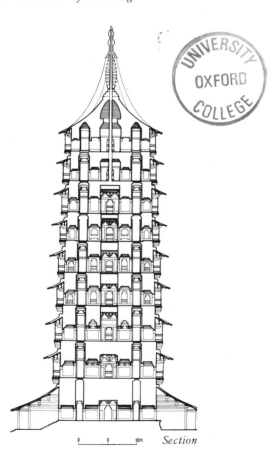

Section

Mañjusrī Hall of Foguang Temple

Wutai   Shanxi   Jin Dynasty   1137 A.D.

By supporting lateral beams with two composite longitudinal girders, four interior columns were spared. The girders are made up of an upper and a lower architrave joined with bracing beams and cog-wheel struts in between, resembling the parallel-chord truss in present-day construction. It was a brave attempt by ancient workers at structural innovation.

Interior view

UNIVERSITY
OXFORD
COLLEGE

Double-layered architrave

Mural at Lingyan Temple

Fanshi Shanxi Jin Dynasty 1167 A.D.

Mañjuśrī Hall of Lingyan Temple was built in the Jin Dynasty. Part of the building was repaired during the Yuan and Ming dynasties. The colorful wall pictures on the east and west walls and part of the north wall are original works done in the Jin Dynasty. In these Buddhist paintings, palaces, city walls, pagodas, galleries, mills, bridges and houses are depicted in details and with precision. They are an important source for the study of Jin architecture.

Liuhe Pagoda

Hangzhou Zhejiang Southern Song Dynasty 1153-1163 A.D.

Situated at Yuelun Peak of Dragon Mountain (Longshan) in Hangzhou, the pagoda overlooks the Qiantang River. It was said that sail boats at night relied on the lights of the pagoda for direction. The pagoda was a seven-story, octagonal building originally; the 13 layers of wooden eaves as we can see now were added in the Guang Xu period during the Qing Dynasty. The xumi style base of the temple still retains scores of Song ornamental carving.

Panorama

110

Sculptures on the xumi *base*

Sanqing Hall of Xuanmiao Temple

Suzhou   Jiangsu   Southern Song Dynasty   1176 A.D.

Built in the Northern Song Dynasty, the original building, called Tianqing Temple, was destroyed in a fire. The present Xuanmiao Temple is a reconstruction of the temple from Southern Song times. The Sanqing Hall (Hall of the Three Pure Ones) is the main building, with a xieshan roof and double eaves. The lower layer is divided into nine bays widthwise and six bays lengthwise. Portions below the ceiling still retain the original Song structure.

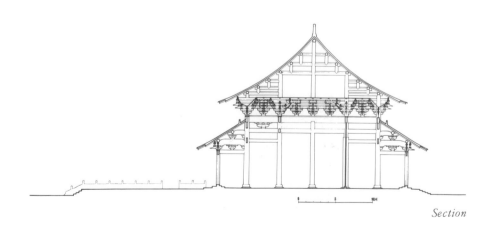

Section

Interior view

UNIVERSITY OXFORD COLLEGE

Main hall of Shang Huayan Temple

Datong   Shanxi   Jin Dynasty   1140 A.D.

   *Consisting of nine bays totaling 53.9 meters in length
and five bays amounting to 27.5 meters in width, this hall
is the largest ancient single-eave timber building.*

Exterior view of the main hall

Shanhua Temple

Datong Shanxi Liao and Jin dynasties 11-12 century

The main gate, Sansheng Hall, Puxian Hall and the main hall are the four major buildings of the temple still in existence. Apart from the main hall, which was constructed in the Liao Dynasty (916-1125), all were built in the Jin Dynasty (1115-1234). A comparatively old compound, each building had its own characteristics, and by comparing it with other Liao architectural works found in Datong, we can discern the architectural development of the period.

Lugou Qiao (Marco Polo Bridge)

Beijing   Jin Dynasty   1192 A.D.

The bridge, located on the Yongding River ten miles southwest of Beijing, was built in the third year of the Ming Chang period of the Jin Dynasty (1115-1234). It was rebuilt and repaired in the Yuan, Ming and Qing dynasties. It is a large arch-bridge which is eight meters in width, 265 meters in length and consists of eleven arches. Each arch is 16 meters in height and has a span of 16 meters. At present, the bridge is still in good condition and can handle lorries with a carrying capacity of 429 tons.

It was from here that Japanese imperialism intensified its aggression in China on 7 July, 1937. The Marco Polo Bridge Incident marked the beginning of the courageous effort of the Chinese to resist Japanese aggression.

Jiangdong Bridge

Zhangzhou Fujian Southern Song Dynasty 1237-1240 A.D.

Also called Hudu Bridge, it is made of stone with 15 arches. Three stone beams were laid to constitute the bridge surface of each arch. The largest beam has a length of 23.7 meters, a width of 1.32 meters and a height of 1.35 meters, and the weight of this beam amounts to 118 tons. Under conditions of primitive technology, the success of building a bridge across the river and laying down such large component parts shows the unusual wisdom of Chinese builders.

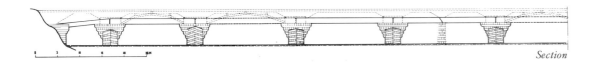

Section

116

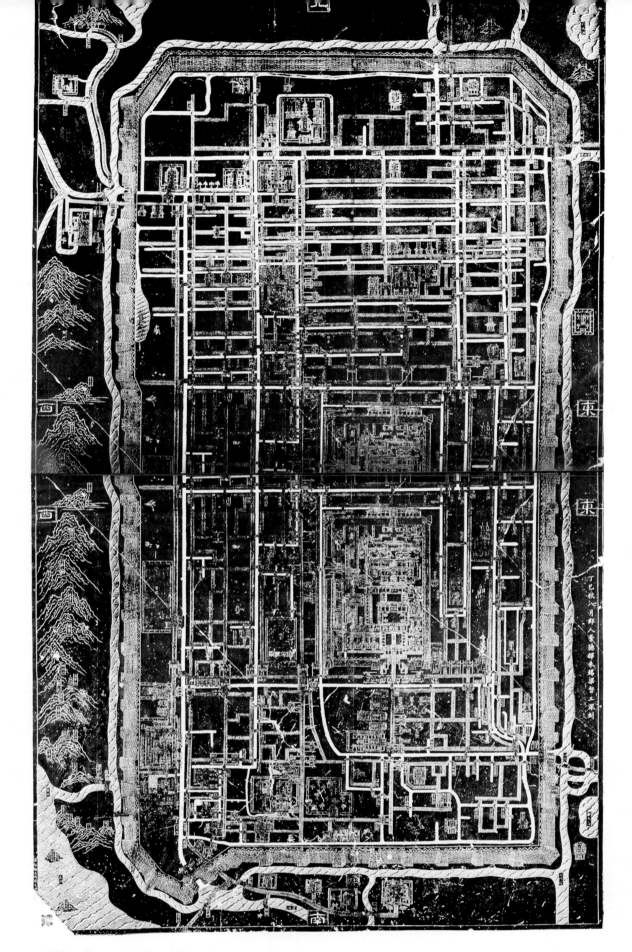

UNIVERSITY
OXFORD
COLLEGE

A Plan-figure stele of Pingjiang in the
Song Dynasty

Suzhou   Jiangsu   Southern Song Dynasty   1229 A.D.

   A work of the Southern Song Dynasty, this carved stele
is 2.02 meters high and 1.36 meters wide. It features a plan
drawing of Pingjiang prefectural city (present-day Suzhou),
clearly showing the location of the government buildings, the
layout of streets and lanes, the city wall, the moat, the
bridges and temples. It also reflects the characteristics and
standards of urban design of the southern cities of the Song
Dynasty.

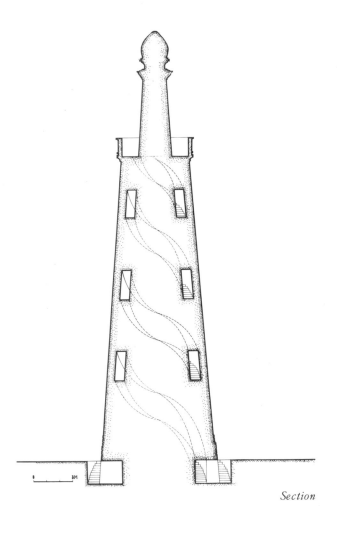

Section

Guang Ta (Minaret) of Huaisheng Temple

Guangzhou Guangdong Southern Song Dynasty 12th century

   In this circular shaped, brick Islamic minaret there are
two doors on the south and north sides of the lowest story.
Inside the minaret are two precisely constructed spiral stairs
opposite each other which lead to the top of the building.
The outer wall of the pagoda has no decoration but is
painted white, rendering a radiant effect.

Main hall

The two pagodas of Kaiyuan Temple
Quanzhou   Fujian   Southern Song Dynasty
1237 A.D. (West Pagoda)   1250 A.D. (East Pagoda)

The two pagodas are located before the main hall of the temple. They are five-storied and eight-sided and located some 200 meters spart. The brackets, beams and the carvings demonstrate the delicacy of the regional method of wood construction. The West Pagoda, often called Renshou Pagoda, and the East Pagoda, called Zhenguo Pagoda, are 44.06 meters and 48.24 meters in height respectively, the latter being the highest stone building in China.

The main hall was rebuilt in the Song Dynasty, and the convexly fluted pillars inside the hall are that of the Song Dynasty.

Panorama

Lowest floor of the East Pagoda

Yongle Palace
Ruicheng Shanxi 1244-1262 A.D.

Yongle Palace was originally situated at the side of the Yellow River in Yongle City, Yongji County, Shanxi Province. When the Sanmen Gorge hydrological project was under construction, the palace was moved to the northern outskirts of Ruicheng.

Along the central axis of Yongle Palace are, from south to north, Wuji Gate, Sanqing Hall, Chunyang Hall and Chongyang Hall. Flanked by no side-halls this was an unusual layout. The walls of four buildings are covered with exquisite frescos from the Yuan Dynasty. Each building has a different plan suited to its particular requirements. Pillars are arranged in such a way as to ensure the proper placing of the statuary without obstructing the views of the frescos. To avoid breaking up the frescos, windows were dispensed with. Instead, adequate daylight is admitted through extensive lattice windows which form the upper part of screen doors on the front facade.

External view of Sanqing Hall

Internal view of Sanqing Hall

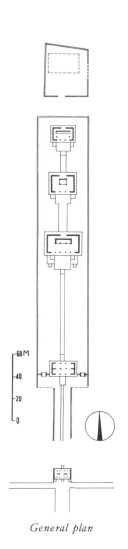

General plan

Wuji Gate

123

White Pagoda of Miaoying Temple

Beijing   Yuan Dynasty   1279 A.D.

 · *It was said that the pagoda was designed by a Nepalese. The pagoda is white in color and built of brick, revealing the special architectural characteristics of Lamaism. It was not until the Yuan Dynasty that this kind of building appeared in north and central China. Imposing and magnificent, it is an outstanding example of Yuan Lamaist pagodas.*

Guanxing Tai (Star Observation Platform)

Dengfeng   Henan   Yuan Dynasty   1276 A.D.

The observatory was constructed by the famous astronomer Guo Shoujing of the Yuan Dynasty, who set out to use it to revise the calendar. It consists of a stone graduated level scale (gui) and a 9.46 meter high platform upon which a cross-bar was placed. At the northern end of the platform is a niche. From the base of the niche the stone graduated scale — Sky Measuring Scale (liangtian chi) — stretches north. At noon, the shadow of the cross-bar would fall on the stone scale. By observing the length of the shadow, the altitude of the sun could be ascertained. Accuracy in lineal measurement of the shadow was within ±2 millimeters.

UNIVERSITY OXFORD COLLEGE

Main Hall of Zhenru Temple

Shanghai Yuan Dynasty 1320 A.D.

This hall has a width of 13.4 meters and a depth of 13 meters The ceiling level of the interior was given different treatments according to functional needs. In the left, right and front sections flat ceiling boards comprise level ceilings while at the back part inclined and vertical struts form a triangulated roof frame so as to enlarge the interior space.

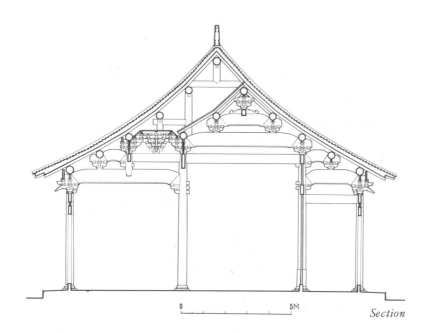

Section

Exterior view

Cloud Terrace of Juyong Guan
Beijing   Yuan Dynasty   1345 A.D.

The Cloud Terrace is situated inside the garrison city of
Juyong Guan northwest of Beijing. It was originally the site
of a Lamaist monastery, the Guojie Pagoda. It is rectangular
in shape, 26.84 meters long and 17.57 meters wide and
built of stone. In the center is a pentagonal archway
entrance, the inner lining and facing of which are of white
marble, exquisitely carved in bas relief and inscribed with
the Dhâraṇî Tantra sūtras in six languages, including
Chinese, Mongolian and Sanskrit.

A Yuan stage

Linfen Shanxi Yuan Dynasty 1345 A.D.

Ancient Chinese opera had its origin in the Tang Dynasty and matured in the Yuan as a popular art form. In its early phase, opera took place on a temporary stage and it was not until under the Song Dynasty that any permanent stage was used. The illustration shows the stage at Dongyue Temple of the Yuan Dynasty in Dongyang Village, Linfen District, Shanxi Province.

Qingjing Temple

Quanzhou Fujian
Yuan Dynasty 1341-1368 A.D

This is a comparatively old Chinese Islamic monastery. The front door is constructed of granite, 20 meters high and 4.5 meters wide. The brackets, arched ceiling, windows, and arabesque inscriptions of both the front door and the sacrifice hall manifest the building style of Islam. They also reflect the long history of cultural interchange between China and other countries.

Main gate

West Wall of the Sacrifice Hall

Tuglug Temür's Tomb

Huocheng   Xinjiang   Yuan Dynasty   1363 A.D.

   Tuglug Temür was a descendent of Genghis Khan. His tomb was built entirely of brick and has a domed roof of 9.7 meters. The building facade is decorated with patterns and Arabic script laid with purple, white and blue colored mosaic tiles.

The Architecture of Feudal Society
Late Period (1368-1840 A.D.)

The Great Wall in the Ming Dynasty

Ming Dynasty 1368-1644 A.D.

The history of the Great Wall can be traced back to the fourth century B.C. During the Warring States Period (475-221 B.C.), protective city walls were built by feudal lords on their fiefs. When China was united by the Qin Dynasty in 221 B.C. the city walls of the former feudal states of Qin, Zhao and Yan were connected. The Great Wall, stretching from Lintao in the west to Liaodong in the east, was thus formed. It was repaired and rebuilt during subsequent dynasties.

The present Great Wall was completed in the Ming Dynasty. Beginning at Jiayu Guan in the west, it stretches over four thousand kilometers to Shanhai Guan in the east. With some sections built of rammed earth and others with brick or stone facing, the Wall has an average height of 7.5 meters. Garrison watchtowers were built at the beginning and end of the walls, at communication nodes and at mountain ravines, examples being the Shanhai Guan, Jiayu Guan, Yanmen Guan, Pingxing Guan and Juyong Guan, the latter built in 1455 A.D. during the first year of the Jing Tai reign. Spanning over rugged terrain, linking garrisons and cities, it is a stupendous engineering project of most impressive grandeur.

The Great Wall is a masterpiece of ancient China. It manifests the tough, determined, and unwavering spirit of the Chinese, and the brightness of the wisdom of the working people.

Garrison watchtower on the
Great Wall

Jiayu Guan

Beijing City in the Ming and Qing periods
Beijing Ming and Qing dynasties post 1368

Beijing had been the capital of the Liao, Jin, Yuan, Ming and Qing dynasties. During the early Ming Dynasty it was rebuilt and extended on the foundation of Dadu City of the Yuan Dynasty. In the 33rd year of the Jia Jing reign (1544 A.D.) of the Ming Dynasty, the Outer City was built, its total area amounting to 60 square kilometers.

The height of the city wall of the Inner City is 12 meters. There is a tower at each corner and each "gate" (men) has a wengcheng (protective quarter outside the main gate), a watchtower, battlements and a gate-tower. Along the main roads inside the Inner City were built brick-paved sewers.

The layout of the city is consistently orthogonal. The Gate of Consolidation (Yongding Men), the Front Gate (Qian Men) and the Gate of Heavenly Peace (Tian'an Men) join the central axis of the Forbidden City and stretch straight north to Jing Hill (Jing Shan), the Drum Tower (Gu Lou) and the Bell Tower (Zhong Lou), forming a grand central axis of eight kilometers which provides the dominant feature of Beijing city.

Watchment and battlements at Zhengyang Men.

Drum Tower and Bell Tower

Wu Men

The Forbidden City of the Ming and Qing periods
Beijing   Ming and Qing dynasties   post 1406 A.D.

The Forbidden City (Zijin Cheng), also known as the Former Palace (Gu Gong), has been the residence of 24 emperors of the Ming and Qing dynasties. Built in the fourth year of the Yong Le reign of the Ming Dynasty, it was expanded and rebuilt many times during the Ming and Qing dynasties, and yet the original layout is preserved. It occupies an area of 73 hectares, extending 960 meters from south to north and 960 meters from east to west. The 9,000 buildings spread over a total area of some 150,000 square meters comprises the largest ancient building ensemble extant in China. Its unified layout and design were based on the idea of the "supremacy of the emperor".

To cater for the decadent living of the ruling classes, all the arts and crafts of feudal society — namely, brickwork,

metal and wood carving, gilding, painting, lacquering, enameling, jade, stone and shell inlaying, and silk mounting — were meticulously and lavishly applied to such constructional elements as beams, corbel brackets, ceiling coffers, door and window traceries, ornamental architraves, decorative balustrades, etc. Thereby, the high level and unique character of ornamentation in classical Chinese architecture was realized.

The central gate of the Forbidden City is Wu Men, also known as the "Five Phoenixes Hall (Wufeng Lou)". Its parapet assumes a ⊓ shape. In the middle are nine towers with double-eaved hipped roofs while at the four corners are square pavilions with double eaves.

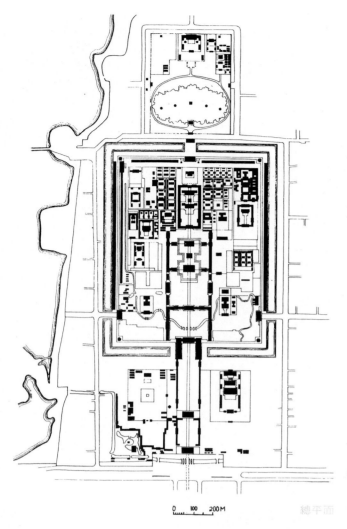

General plan of the Forbidden City

總平面

0 100 200M

Taihe Men

Taihe, Zhonghe and Baohe are the Three Great Halls of the Forbidden City. They are built on a seven-meter high common podium finished in white marble. Both the balustrades and steps are finely decorated with bas-relief.

Taihe Hall was rebuilt during the 34th year of the reign of Kang Xi (1695). Nine bays wide and 35.05 meters high, it is the largest building in the Forbidden City.

Taihe Hall Square

Taihe Hall

*Stone steps flanking the Cloud-and-dragon Ramp
leading to Taihe Hall*

An elegant coffered ceiling in Taihe Hall

Interior view of Taihe Hall

143

Dongnuan Pavilion of Yangxin Hall

Yangxin Gate

Constituting a building compound immediately next to the Three Great Halls, the Qianqing Palace, Jiaotai Hall and Kunyu Palace are poised on a common podium. They were built in the 12th year of the Shun Zhi reign (1655) during the Qing Dynasty. To the east of Qianqing Palace are the Jingren Hall, Chengqian Hall, Zhongcui Hall, Yongle Hall, and Jingyang Hall. To the west are Taiji Hall, Tiyuan Hall, Changchun Hall, Yikun Hall, Tihe Hall and Chuxiu Hall. They are called the Six Palaces of the East and West. In front of the West Six Palaces is Yangxin Hall. At the east of the East Six Palaces is Ningzhou Hall. All are extremely lavishly appointed and exquisitely decorated.

Qianqing Palace

Inner view of Yikun Hall

Inner view of Leshou House in Huangji Hall

A corner hall

UNIVERSITY OXFORD COLLEGE

Jing Hill

Jing Hill is situated outside Shenwu Gate north of the Forbidden City. It has five crests, with a pavilion built on top of each. It used to be the highest place in Beijing.

Panorama of the Forbidden City

The Thirteen Mausoleums of Ming

Beijing   Ming Dynasty   1049-1644 A.D.

Thirteen emperors of the Ming Dynasty were buried in Tianshou Mountain in Changping Province, north of Beijing. The place is called Shisan Ling — the Thirteen Mausoleums. The stretch of pavement leading to the mausoleums is seven kilometers long. Along it were placed stone memorial archways, Dahong Gate, pavilions with memorial tablets, eighteen pairs of stone-carved figures and animal statues, Lingxing Gate, and other constructions and carvings. The 28.86 meter wide memorial archway of white marble with five gates, six pillars and eleven stories is the largest stone archway in China. The stone animals were carved out of single pieces of rock, the largest one being 30 cubic meters in volume.

Animal statues

Stone memorial archway

Chang Ling, mausoleum of Emperor Cheng Zu, is the largest among the Thirteen Mausoleums of the Ming Dynasty. Situated in it is the Ling'en Hall. Nine bays wide, totaling 66.75 meters and five bays deep, totaling 29.31 meters, Ling'en Hall is the largest ancient hall still in existence. The sixty columns supporting the roof of the hall are made of whole Machilus namu tree logs, the diameter of the largest four measuring 1.17 meters.

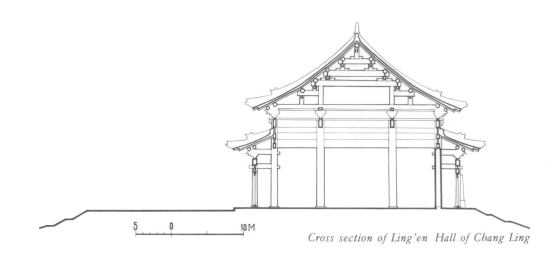

Cross section of Ling'en Hall of Chang Ling

5 0 10 M

Interior view of Ling'en Hall

UNIVERSITY OXFORD COLLEGE

Brilliant Tower (Minglou) *on Square Gatehouse* (Fangcheng) *at Chang Ling*

Underground palace of Ding Ling

Ding Ling, another tomb among the Thirteen Mausoleums, was completed during the reign of Wan Li, and excavated during 1956. It consists of five halls: the front, middle, back, right and left halls, which are all stone-vaulted. Situated 27 meters underground, it has a total area of 1,195 square meters. Large quantities of white marble, polished stone and brick were used in its construction.

Central chamber of the underground hall

154

Jing Ling
Junhua   Hebei   Qing Dynasty   1722 A.D.
Jing Ling is the mausoleum of Emperor Sheng Zu of the
Qing Dynasty.

Qinian Temple

Temple of Heaven

Beijing   Ming and Qing dynasties   since 1420 A.D.

The ensemble of the Temple of Heaven was built in the 18th year of the reign Yong Le of the Ming Dynasty, and has an area of about 270 hectares. The major buildings are Huanqiu Altar, Huangqiong House and Qinian Temple. Huanqiu Altar is a circular marble terrace with a diameter of 55 meters, divided into three levels surrounded by two wall enclosures, the inner one being round and the outer one being square. It was here that the ceremony of "sacrifice to the heavens" took place. Huangqiong House, situated at the north of Huanqiu Altar, is the hall in which the memorial tablet of the "Emperor of Heaven" was placed. Circular in shape and 63 meters in diameter, it is surrounded by a wall. Qinian Temple is the place for "praying for a good harvest". When it was first constructed in the Ming Dynasty, it was a large rectangular hall with eleven sections, but when rebuilt later in 1898, it was changed to a circular shape. With a diameter of 30 meters, the present building stands on a three-level podium of white marble 90 meters in diameter. Totaling 38 meters in height, the whole construction has an imposing and stable look while the interior of the hall, with its coffered ceiling, is finely constructed and colorfully decorated.

UNIVERSITY OXFORD COLLEGE

157

Coffered ceiling of the Qianian Temple

Painted ornaments on the outer architraves of the Qinian Temple

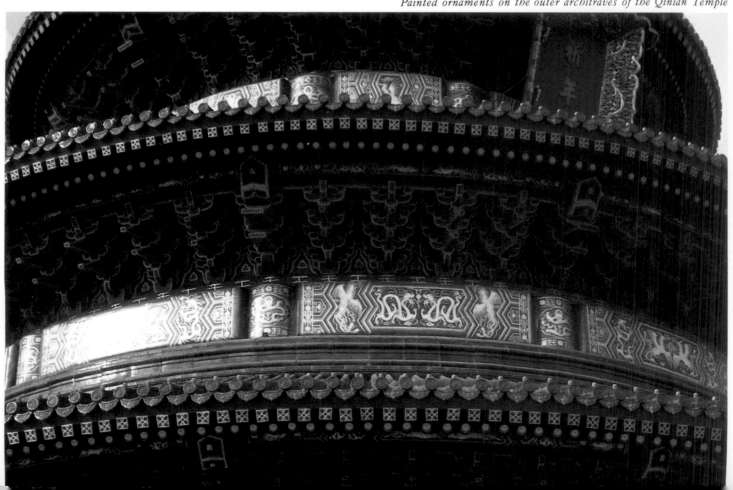

UNIVERSITY OXFORD COLLEGE

Huangqiong House

Coffered ceiling inside Huangqiong House

Bird's-eye view of the Temple of Heaven

161

Main Hall of Linggu Temple

Nanjing   Jiangsu   Ming Dynasty   1376-1382 A.D.

Linggu Temple is at the southern foothill of Zijin Mountain outside the city of Nanjing. Built of brick, the main hall is the largest and earliest ''beamless hall'' in existence. Its 53.8-meter width is made up of three vaults, the middle vault spanning 11.25 meters at a 14 meter height.

Interior view

Close-up view

Pagoda of the Buddha's Seat, Great Enlightenment Temple

Beijing   Ming Dynasty   1473 A.D.

The Great Enlightenment Temple (Dazhengjue Temple) is also called Five Pagodas Temple. The Buddha's Seat (Jingang Baozuo) Pagoda is built of white marble and has a five-meter high podium. On the foundation are also five small rectangular pagodas with solid eaves. The style of construction is said to be based on guidelines given by an Indian monk. The pagoda therefore reveals the characteristics of Indian as well as traditional Chinese architecture, exemplifying the cultural interflow between China and India.

UNIVERSITY OXFORD COLLEGE

Feihong Pagoda of Guangshengshang Temple

Hongdong Shanxi
Ming Dynasty 1515-1527 A.D.

Octagonal in plan, the pagoda is built entirely of brick, faced with glazed tiles of yellow, green, blue and other colors. Historically, Shanxi has been particularly advanced in the making of glaze-ware. This pagoda is one of the fine examples of its application.

Panorama

164

Detail

165

Biyun Temple

Beijing Ming and Qing dynasties

The Biyun Temple is situated at the eastern foothill of West Hill in Beijing, with its six courts built along the spur, one following the other. Śakaymuni Hall, the main building, was erected in the Ming Dynasty, and has an intricately ornamental coffered ceiling. The building at the back is the Buddha's Seat (Jingang Baozu) Pagoda. On the right side of this pagoda still stands the Arhat Hall whose plan resembles the Chinese character tian (田).

When Dr Sun Yat-sen died in Beijing in 1925, his body was temporarily placed inside the Buddha's Seat Pagoda. He was later burried in the mausoleum in Nanjing bearing his name. This pagoda was renamed the Cenotaph of Dr Sun. Inside the temple compound a memorial hall for Sun was also constructed.

Waiba Temples

Chengde Hebei Qing Dynasty 1713-1780 A.D.

During the reigns of Kang Xi and Qian Long emperors of the Qing Dynasty, seven temples were built on the northern foothill of Shizi Gou in Chengde and four others were built on the east bank of the Wulie River. These were commonly known as the "Waiba Temples". Taking full advantage of the terrain, these temples are built on slopes and serve as good examples of how construction can adapt itself to the topography. Some of the temples adopted characteristics of Tibetan architecture, resulting in a creative integration of the architectural styles of the Hans and the Tibetans.

Puning Temple

Under the instigation of the Russians, the Junger Dawači rebelled in 1754 and threatened to dismember the whole Chinese nation. After their suppression by the Qing Dynasty, a banquet was held at the Imperial Summer Resort for the higher nobility of the Elügüt Mongols. Puning Temple was built in 1755 to commemorate the event. The main building at the front is the main hall while at the rear is the Māhāyana Pavilion which is divided into seven bays widthwise. Around the Māhāyana Pavilion are chambers and pavilions as well as Lamaist pagodas faced with glazed tiles of different colors.

UNIVERSITY OXFORD COLLEGE

Lamaist Pavilion of Puning Temple

Mahāyana Pavilion of Puning Temple

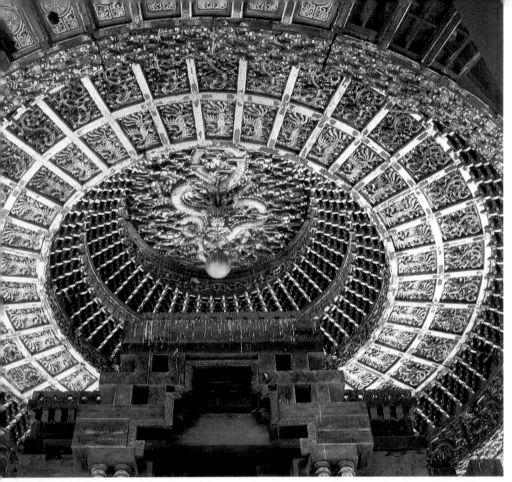

Recessed and coffered ceiling in Yuguang Pavilion of Pule Temple

Pule Temple

Also called Yuan Tingzi (Circular Pavilion), it was built in 1766 A.D. It was specially erected for the leaders of the tribes of the Kazak and Burut, who went to Chengde on their tributary missions and visits. The main building of the front part is the Zongyin Hall while at the rear is the 80 meters long rectangular building Du Cheng. Du Cheng is divided into three levels of construction, and on the uppermost level is built the circular Yuguang Pavilion which is a grand hall with a circular pointed roof and double eaves. The recessed and coffered ceiling of the pavilion is exquisitely constructed.

Anyuan Temple

Anyuan Temple is also called Ili Temple. Built in the year 1764 A.D., its form is based on the Kuldya Kürö, a place of worship of the Junger tribe north of the River Ili in Xinjiang Province.

Pudu Hall of Anyuan Temple

Putuo Zongcheng Temple

During the Qian Long reign, after the suppression of the Junger rebellion, the upper class people of the tribes south and north of the desert area in Northwest China and those in Qinghai and Xinjiang provinces gathered in Chengde. This indicated a wish for unification among the tribes. The Qing government valued this event highly, and built this temple as an imitation of the Lamaist center of the country — the Potala Palace in Lhasa. The temple was completed in 1771 and occupied an area of 220,000 square meters. The front part of the construction has a clear central axis while at the rear a number of flat-roofed Tibetan style houses were laid out more freely to follow the natural topography. The last major building compound comprises the Wanfaguiyi Temple and its surrounding buildings. The wall is painted with a red wash and is called Dahong Tai (Red Terrace). The roofs of the pavilions on the top of Wanfaguiyi Temple and other buildings are covered with gilded copper tiles. Sparkling among the red wall and colored glazes, the gilded copper tiles constitute a magnificent sight.

UNIVERSITY OXFORD COLLEGE

173

Glazed memorial archway of Putuo Zongcheng Temple

Red Terrace of Putuo
Zongcheng Temple

Xumi Fushou Temple

   Built in 1780, the temple is an imitation of the
Trashilungpo Monastery in Xigazê. It is smaller than the
Putuo Zongcheng Temple, but the buildings are more
centralized. The major structure, the Red Terrace, is
situated at the center of the complex. The building at the
back of the temple is an opulent octagonal seven story glazed
pagoda.

Miaogao Zhuangyan Hall of the Temple

Bird's-eye view of the Xumi Fushou Temple

UNIVERSITY
OXFORD
COLLEGE

Red Terrace and Memorial Archway of Xumi Fushou Temple

UNIVERSITY OXFORD COLLEGE

Potala Palace

Lhasa Tibet Qing Dynasty 1645 A.D.

Situated on a hilltop to the west of Lhasa, this building is large and grand. One of the most spectacular structures in Tibet, it was built by the great Tibetan leader Songtsan Gampo in the seventh century. The existing buildings were begun in the second year of the Shun Zhi reign in the Qing Dynasty. More than seven thousand slaves were forced to take part in the construction every day, and it took more than 50 years to complete the whole project. The palace is constructed of stone and wood, 15 stories at the highest point and over 400 meters long from east to west. It has over 15,000 rooms of different sizes. All of the buildings are flat-roofed while on the top of the highest buildings are built three grand halls with wudian (hipped) and xieshan (half-hipped, half-gabled) styles of roofs which are covered with gilded copper tiles.

UNIVERSITY OXFORD COLLEGE

180

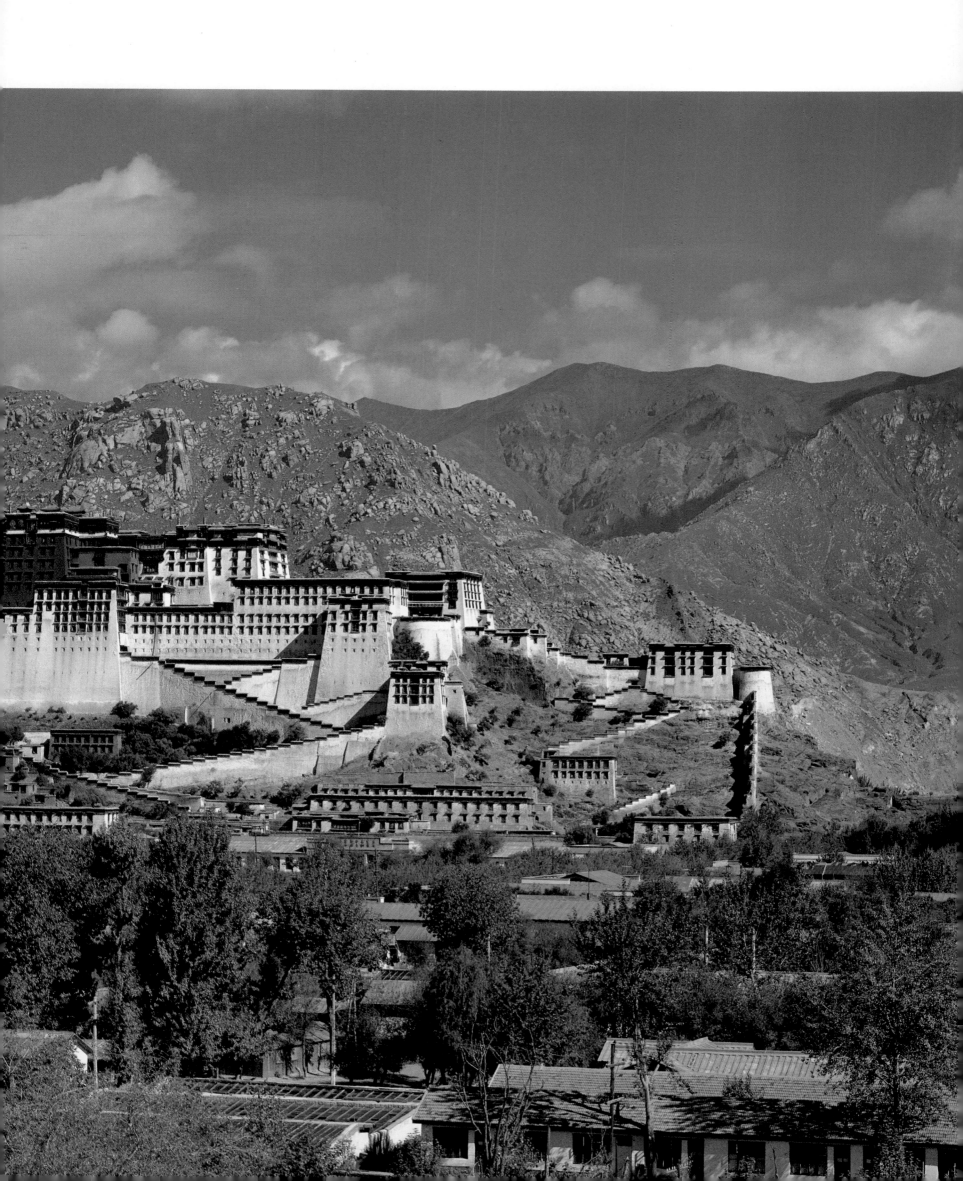

Trashilungpo Monastery

Xigazê   Tibet   Ming Dynasty   post 1447 A.D.

One of the six most famous lamaseries, the monastery
was built in the Ming Dynasty and was rebuilt in subsequent
years. The Cuoqing Palace and the fresco of the palace are
products of the Ming. This is one of the earliest palaces to
be completed in the monastery.

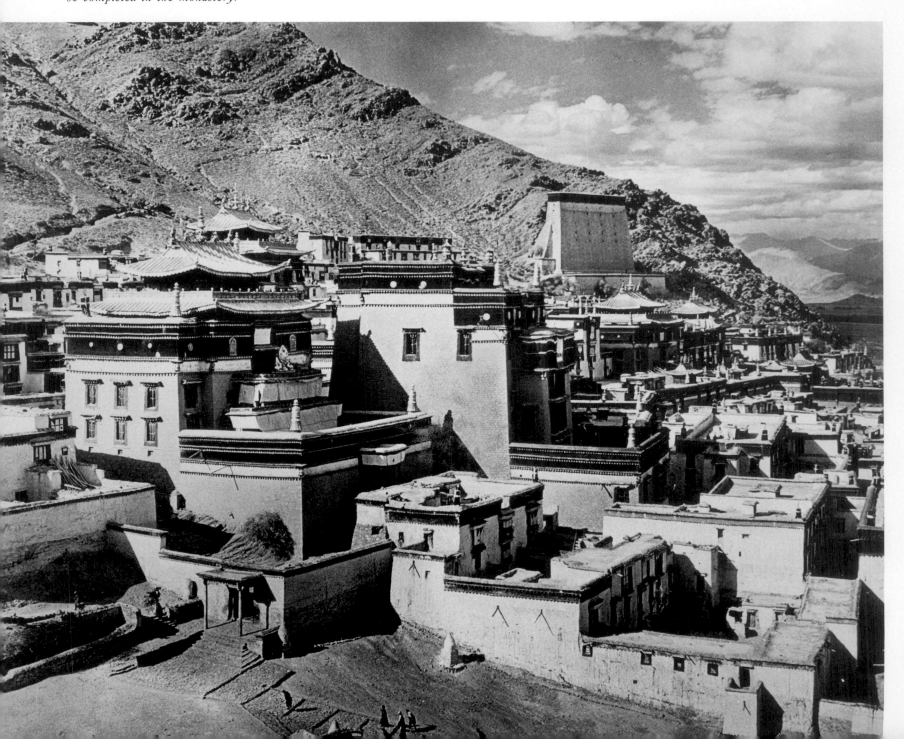

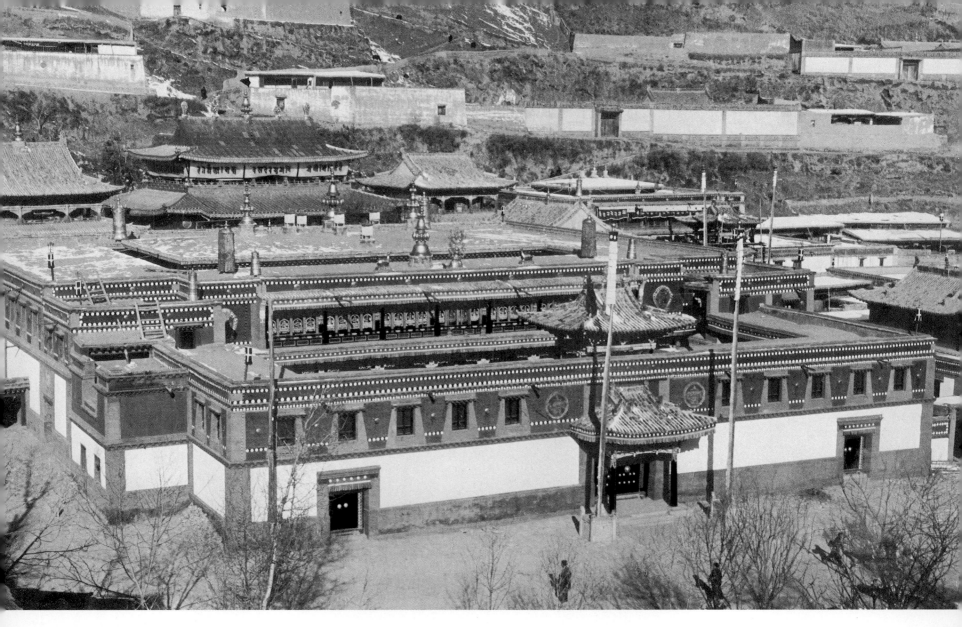

Kumbum Monastery

Huangzhong Qinghai Qing Dynasty 18th century

Huangzhong of Qinghai Province was the native place of Tsonghkapa, who was the leader of the Gelu Sect (Yellow Sect) of Lamasiam. The Kumbum Monastery at the southern part of Huangzhong is one of the six most famous lama-series. Most of the construction and design of the temple was adopted from the building techniques of the Han Chinese.

UNIVERSITY OXFORD COLLEGE

Shireetü Dzuu

*Hohhot Inner Mongolia Qing Dynasty
1696 A.D.*

Along the central axis of this lamasery are five buildings. The major one, Da Jingtang (Main Worshipping Hall), is nine bays wide and nine bays deep. Inside the hall are many pillars covered with yellow and blue striped tapestries. In the front is a gallery with seven sections. On the top, the roof consists of a sloping and a flat surface covered with yellow glazed tiles and decorated with gilded copper designs. The wall of the hall is faced with blue glazed bricks, typical of a Mongolian lamasery.

Interior view of Da Jingtang

Exterior view of Da Jingtang

Xiong Jin Stupas

Ruili   Yunnan   Qing Dynasty

In monasteries of the Dai people, the parallel construction of a hall and a group of stupas comprises the major structure. Such a group of stupas is usually elegantly shaped and rich in beautiful carvings. The Xiong Jin Stupas are a good example. The base of this group of stupas is a complicated structure in the shape of the Chinese character ya (亞). The main stupa has a slim body, surrounded by smaller stupas and statues of animals.

UNIVERSITY OXFORD COLLEGE

Dai Monasteries

Qing Dynasty

The halls of monasteries of the Dai people living in the villages of Yunnan Province are usually rectangular with tile roofs and arranged on a north-south axis. The top descends successively in three or five tiers. On the beams and pillars of the monastery are pictures painted in gold and red, an ethnic characteristic of the Dai. The stupas are usually circular or polygonal and are similar to those found in Burma and Thailand.

Amin Stupa and Worshipping Hall

Turpan Xinjiang Qing Dynasty 1778 A.D.

During the reign of Qian Long, Amin Khoja, an upper class member of the Uygur nationality, by opposing the reactionary leader of the Junger people who conspired with the Russians in an attempt to dismember China, contributed to the preservation of the empire. This edifice was built to commemorate him. The worshipping hall is made of mud brick and the walls are protected with lime, giving them a silvery white appearance. The Amin Stupa, 44 meters high, was constructed of greyish-green bricks which are also used to form a beautiful pattern on the outer wall of the whole construction. Inside the stupa is a flight of spiral steps laid in brick.

UNIVERSITY OXFORD COLLEGE

187

Atikar Mosque

Kashgar Xinjiang Ming Dynasty post 14th century

On the right and left side before the central gate of the mosque are two circular minarets. The worshipping hall, which faces the main entrance, is thirty-eight bays wide, rare among ancient building. It is of hypostyle hall design, and the secondary beams of the flat ceiling are formed into various patterns, emphasized by colorful painting. Four three-bay deep ancillary buildings inside the hall account for the projection of its central portion. Eight brick inner halls which face these ancillary buildings are used by worshippers in the winter.

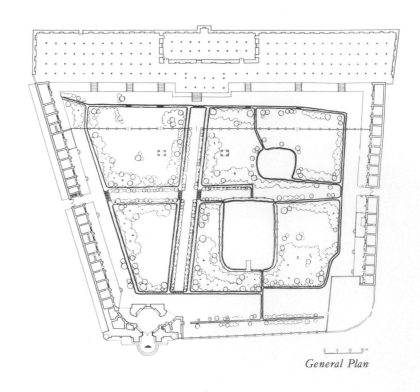

General Plan

Worshipping Hall

UNIVERSITY OXFORD COLLEGE

*Decorations of plaster stone
in the Worshipping Hall*

189

Huangshi Imperial Archive

Beijing Ming Dynasty 1534 A.D.

Structurally, Huangshi Imperial Archive is of cylindrical brick and stone vaulting. There are two doors. The door leaves of the outer door are made of stone. installed inside is a white marble xumi seat (a kind of base in Chinese architecture, usually elaborately carved). On the seat there are the 20 wooden cabinets which were used to keep documents. The wooden cabinets are sheathed in copper leaf with a ''cloud and dragon'' pattern. They are commonly known as the ''Golden Cabinets (Jingui)''. During the Ming Dynasty, a duplicate copy of the Yong Le Dadian (Encyclopaedia of Yong Le) was stored here. Later, it was used to keep important documents such as the Imperial Chronology of Major Events, and the Royal Instructions and Genealogy of the Royal Family. It is the oldest national archive.

Exterior view

Tianyi Pavilion

Ningbo Zhejiang Ming Dynasty 16th century

During the Ming Dynasty this was the private library of a Fan family of Ningbo. The room is divided into six bays and has two stories. Both at the rear and the front of the building are ponds and artificial mountains, creating a quiet environment. Because the building was utilized for book storage, special attention was paid in the design to the prevention of fire and the control of pests and moisture. As a result, the structure is well preserved up to present. When Qian Long of the Qing Dynasty edited the Siku quanshu (The Qing Encyclopaedia), Tianyi Pavilion was used as a model for the building of Wenyuan Pavilion (where the Siku quanshu was stored) and five other archives.

Interior view

Dacheng Hall of Confucian Temple

Tainan   Taiwan   Qing Dynasty

   Built in the 19th year of the Yong Li reign of the
Southern Ming Dynasty (1665), this was the earliest
Confucian temple built in Taiwan. It was rebuilt in the Qing
Dynasty. The temple includes Dacheng Hall, Minglun Hall,
Wenchang Pavilion and other buildings. Adjacent to the
temple are gardens and courts, well planted with lush
vegetation such as old banyan trees which almost conceal
the sky. It was said that one of the old willows was planted
by Zheng Chenggong, the general who continued to resist
the Qing after the collapse of the Ming Dynasty.

Yinping Bridge

Wenxian Gansu Qing Dynasty

For bridges across steep ravines and rapids, the working people in China used a cantilever type of wooden bridge. Logs were corbelled out from the two sides of the river bank and connected in the middle by wooden beams. In this way, bridge piers and supporting columns were dispensed with. Though the cantilever wooden bridges in Gansu, Fujian,, Qinghai and Guangxi are contemporary structures, they reflect the bridge building method of ancient China. Yinping Bridge is one such example.

UNIVERSITY OXFORD COLLEGE

Chengyang Bridge

Sanjiang   Guangxi   Qing Dynasty

In the rainy and humid region of southern China, timber bridges are often roofed over with long galleries. Known as "rain and wind" bridges or covered bridges, they not only provide shelter to users, but also afford protection to the structural timber. The multiple-eaved gallery over the Chengyang Bridge in Guangxi exhibits the unique building characteristics of the Dong nationality.

Luding Bridge

Luding   Sichuan   Qing Dynasty   1701 A.D.

Luding Bridge is an iron-chain suspension bridge 103.7 meters long and about 3 meters wide. Nine iron chains were fastened to the two sides of the river banks and covered with wood planks, while two other chains were used as railings. Stone abutments on both banks anchor the ends of the iron chains, a feature typical of traditional bridge construction in China's mountainous southwest.

In May 1935, when the Red Army reached Luding Bridge during the Long March, they were intercepted by their enemy. Twenty heroes of the poineer section dashed to the iron chain bridge and laid down new wooden planks. These enabled the crossing of the river and gained victory in the famous "War of Luding Bridge".

UNIVERSITY OXFORD COLLEGE

Overhanging Temple

Hunyuan   Shanxi   Qing Dynasty

   The whole temple juts out from a rock cliff face and is reached by trestle-gallery road. At the back side of the temple is the cliff while the front faces a steep slope. Being built on the middle of the mountain, the temple construction was very difficult and dangerous.

Hall of the Mansion on Bridge

Jingxing Hebei Qing Dynasty

Hall of the Mansion on Bridge (Qiulou Dian) is a monastic compound situated on Cangyan Mountain 40 kilometers south of Jingxing. The main hall is built at the side of a ravine, and the two affiliated halls are set on an arch bridge spanning the gulch. It is an example of how ancient Chinese workers were able to take appropriate measures to cope with local conditions. This construction of buildings on a bridge across a chasm demonstrates the precision of their constructional techniques.

Residential buildings in various districts
Ming and Qing dynasties

A vast country comprising many nationalities, China has a complex topography and climate. In building their dwellings the ancient Chinese showed their architectural talents in meeting local conditions with appropriate measures. As a result, buildings in different styles and structures flourished.

In North China, Northeast China and the Northwest Plain living compounds enclosed by houses on three or four sides flourished. Along the rivers and streets south of the Yangtze River were row houses, while in Fujian and Guangzhou the Kejia people lived together in communal dwellings. In mountainous regions where the population was sparse there were detached houses. All are examples of house types developed in reponse to real-life requirements.

Structures of the buildings also differed as a result of variations in natural environments and living customs. Houses of the Han people were generally of timber tiered beam or tenoned beam frame construction, and shapes of the roofs ranged from sloping and arched to flat. In mountainous regions where the supply of timber was plentiful, walls were built of horizontal timbering. In rainy and damp regions houses were built on stilts. In the Huangtu Plateau in West Henan and North Shaanxi people lived in cave dwellings, while in Inner Mongolia and Xinjiang where people roamed the steppes, settling where there was grass and water, they

devised the yurt and the tent which were easily demountable. In dry and hot Turpan, domestic buildings were commonly flat-topped and of sun-dried mud brick, and in mountainous Qinghai and Tibet flat-topped stone houses were prevalent.

Walls of the buildings also varied in their structures. Besides brick, there were many other types. The rammed-earth double-layered wall was popular in West Fujian where buildings might be three stories high. In Guangdong walls as high as four stories were made of pebblestones, while in Yunnan they were usually of bamboo slats woven in beautiful design patterns. In Shaoxing and Tiantai in Zhejiang Province, stone slabs were used. In other regions south of the Yangtze River, walls were either made of hollow bricks or wattle walls of grass and earth with timber struts. All these show the advanced level of the builders' craft among ordinary Chinese people in the past.

Lu Xun's Residence at Beijing

A quadrangular courthouse (sihe yuan) *at Beijing*

199

Residences in Taigu, Shanxi

Cave dwelling in Shanxi

Houses in Shangrao, Jiangxi

UNIVERSITY
OXFORD
COLLEGE

Houses in Hangzhou, Zhejiang

Residences in Wenling, Zhejiang

A residence in Yongding, Fujian

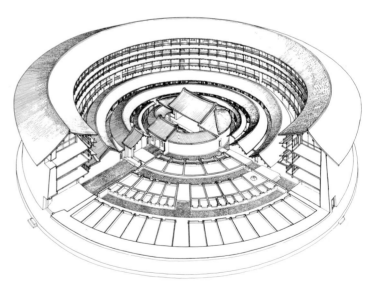

Anatomic view of the residence in Yongding

Residences in Nan'an, Fujian

A residence in Jinjiang, Fujian

Houses of the Miao people in Rongshui, Guangxi

UNIVERSITY OXFORD COLLEGE

205

Houses of the Dong people in Sanjiang, Guangxi

Houses of the Yao people in Longshan, Guangxi

UNIVERSITY
OXFORD
COLLEGE

Residences in Meixian, Guangdong

Residences in Rongjiang, Guizhou

Houses of the Naxi people in Lijiang, Yunnan

Houses of the Dai people in Ruili, Yunnan

208

UNIVERSITY OXFORD COLLEGE

Residences of the Tibetan in Lhasa, Tibet

Tibetan residences in Xiahe, Gansu

Site of Fanghu scenic spot

Site of Yuan Ming Garden
Beijing   Qing Dynasty   1709-1860

Yuan Ming Garden was situated at the northwestern part of Beijing. It consisted of three parks, namely Yuan Ming Garden, Chang Chun Garden and Wanchun Garden, and was therefore also named the Three Gardens, with a perimeter of about ten kilometers and an area of 300 hectares. In it, there were thousands of pavilions, terraces, houses, cottages and palaces, including imitations of the gardens of the south and natural scenery of that region. No wonder it was reputed to be "The Garden of Gardens". Every building was beautifully appointed and well adorned with precious antiques, works of art and valuable ornaments. This world famous garden was twice raided by the foreigners, once during the Anglo-French expedition of 1860 and again during the eight-nation expedition of 1900, as result of which only ruins remain.

Shangxia Tianguang

UNIVERSITY OXFORD COLLEGE

Bitong College

Panorama of Yihe Garden

Yihe Garden (Summary Palace)

Beijing   Qing Dynasty   post 1702 A.D.

During the early Qing Dynasty, Emperor Kang Xi chose the northwestern suburb of Beijing, a scenic region since the Yuan and Ming, as the site for the Wengshan imperial traveling lodge, which was later renamed Qingyi Garden.

In 1860, during the Anglo-French expedition, the garden was burnt down and was reconstructed by the Empress Dowager in 1888 with funds originally intended for the navy and renamed Yihe Garden (commonly known to the West as the Summer Palace). The garden was again raided by the eight-nation expedition in 1900 and repaired in 1903, but the high grounds at the rear never recovered their original appearance.

The total area of the garden is about 3.4 square kilo-meters, of which three quarters are covered by water. The garden mainly consists of Mount Weng and the lake. In the eastern part is the imperial resort of the Qing emperors, while in the lake area are the Dragon King Temple, the seventeen-arch bridge, West Dam as well as islands and pagodas in imitation of the West Lake in Hangzhou. The mountain is at the north, and along the central axis which linked up the foot and the top of the hill are Paiyun Hall, Foxiang Hall, Zhihuihai Temple, etc. On the foothill by the side of the lake are 273 galleries. Besides these, there are smaller detached gardens which are quasi replicas of the gardens in the Yangtze region. For example, Xiequ Garden is an imitation of Jichang Garden of the Wuxi District.

Seventeen Arch Bridge

Foxiang Hall

UNIVERSITY OXFORD COLLEGE

Zhihuihai Temple

A gallery

Yudai Bridge

UNIVERSITY OXFORD COLLEGE

Duobao Glazed Pagoda

Xiequ Garden

218

UNIVERSITY OXFORD COLLEGE 219

Bei Hai Park

Beijing   Ming and Qing dynasties

Also called Taiye Chi, it was a famous scenic ground and traveling lodge for the emperor during the Liao and Jin dynasties. In the Yuan Dynasty, it was incorporated into the western part of the Imperial City. Rebuilt and repaired in the Ming and Qing periods to a total area of 60 hectares, Bei Hai encompasses a vast lake in the southern part of which is the Qionghua Island with its white Lamaist pagoda. On the northern end of Qionghua Island sixty galleries are linked to halls from which the Five Dragon Pavilions (Wulong Ting) across the water to the north may be viewed. On the northern and eastern banks of the lake are Nine Dragon Wall (Jiulong Bi), Jingxin Study, Haopu Jian Pavilions and numerous other minor gardens.

Panorama of Qionghua Island

UNIVERSITY OXFORD COLLEGE

Five Dragon Pavilions facing Qinghua Island to its south

*Northern gallery of
Qionghua Island*

Nine Dragon Wall

UNIVERSITY OXFORD COLLEGE

Detail of Nine Dragon Wall

Imperial Summer Resort

Chengde   Hebei   Qing Dynasty
post 1703 A.D.

Built in the 42nd year of the
reign of Kang Xi and extended in
the Qian Long period, it has a
perimeter of about 20 li (10,800
meters). The hilly region to the
northwest occupies four-fifths of
the total area while to the southeast is a plain with lakes. The
knolls, plain, and the lakes in the
area constitute a landscape that
combines the garden making
characteristics of the North and
South. It is the largest classical
garden found in China with an
area of 5,640,000 square meters.

The imperial traveling lodge is
built on level ground on the
southeast foothill, while an official
archive, the Wenjin Repository, is
situated at the foothills to the
east. The large tract of lowlying
grounds at the north bank of the
lake, wooded and stocked with
deer, is called Wanshu Garden
(Ten Thousand Tree Garden).
Inside the garden was the Yongyou
Temple, but now only a nine-story
pagoda of it remains. On the lake
is the Shuixin Pavilion (Lake
Center Pavilion) and several
islands. The layout of the gardens
in the Summer Resort is largely
patterned on gardens of the South.
For example, Wen Garden follows
the design of Shizi Garden in
Suzhou, Jinshan Pavilion is
modeled after Jinshan Temple in
Zhenjiang District, while Yanyu
Mansion resembles a mansion of
the same name in Jiaqing District.

Lake Center Pavilions

UNIVERSITY OXFORD COLLEGE

225

Yanyu Mansion

Portico of Danpo Jincheng Hall

Tibetan Gardens

Lhasa Tibet Qing Dynasty

Norbu Lingka

In Tibetan the name means the "Treasure Garden". Originally it was the summer resort palace of the Dalai Lama. Inside the garden, there are monasteries, lily ponds, pavilions, paths paved in ornamental patterns and various rare animals and birds.

Longwang Lake

Named after the Longwang Temple on its banks, it is located at the back of Potala Mountain and is a scenic resort. On holidays and festivals, many inhabitants of Lhasa find relaxation by boating here.

UNIVERSITY OXFORD COLLEGE

Norbu Lingka

Gardens in the Yangtze region

Ming and Qing dynasties

In Ming and Qing times, pleasure-seeking bureaucrats and rich landowners often artificially created illusions of "natural landscapes in the city" by constructing gardens of man-made ponds and hills around their residences. Private garden were thus very much in vogue at that time. Among those still extant the best-known ones include Zhan Garden in Nanjing, Jichang Garden in Wuxi, Zhuozheng Garden, Liu Garden and Wangshi Garden in Suzhou and Yu Garden in Shanghai.

Private gardens of the Yangtze region were generally small. Yet, within their restricted spaces, traditional garden-makers were able to create a diversity of views. This is achieved by the skilful use of "borrowed landscape", by the partitioning of space, by the interplay of harmony and contrast, and by capturing the essential characteristics of natural landscapes.

The superb handling of water in the gardens of the Yangtze region is well-known. Man-made hills, pavilions, bridges, flowers and trees are carefully placed close to the ponds to produce, in their combination, different moods and vistas of still or rippled water surfaces, or of meandering streams, of illusion or substance, of concentration or dispersal. These water bodies are embellished by the lotus and fish within while brooklets and cascades further enhance one's enjoyment of nature.

In Yangtze gardens, abundant use of stones was made in forming rock crests, cliffs, artificial hills, and lining the edges of ponds. Whether it was in the imitation of a precarious cliff, a precipitous chasm, a mountain range, a valley pass, a rocky cavern, or half-submerged rocks, our artisans of the past followed closely nature's visual characteristics of their geomorphology, texture, pedology, and vegatation, to achieve that illusion of "works of man, yet the appearance of creation".

Gardens of the Yangtze region were mostly in ruins before 1949. After 1949, refurbishing was done and they were reopened as recreation grounds for the people.

Panorama of Zhuozheng Garden

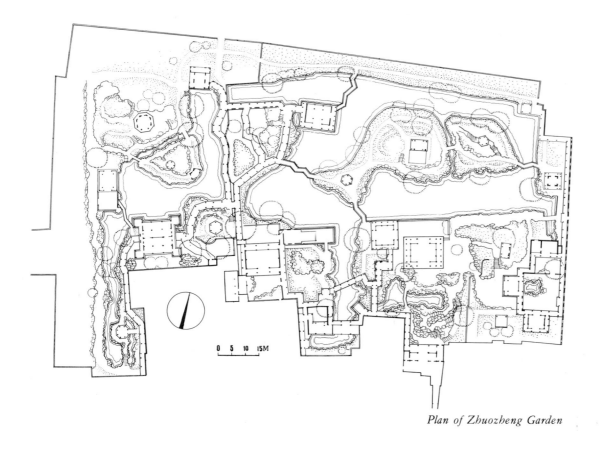

0 5 10 15M

Plan of Zhuozheng Garden

Wuzhu Pavilion of Zhuozheng Garden

Pavilion of Moon Arriving and Breeze Coming, Wangshi Garden

Panorama of Wangshi Garden

231

Quxi House in Liu Garden

He Suo (Garden Court of Cranes) in Liu Garden

UNIVERSITY OXFORD COLLEGE

A lake corridor of Zhuozheng Garden in Suzhou

Lattice windows in the Court of Haitang Chunwu, Wangshi Garden

UNIVERSITY
OXFORD
COLLEGE

A moon gate in Yi Garden

Paved yard in Yi Garden, Suzhou

Artificial rockeries in Zhuozheng Garden

Artificial rockeries in Yu Garden in Shanghai

UNIVERSITY OXFORD COLLEGE

Santan Yinyue (Three Pools Mirroring the Moon) in Hangzhou

Appendices

A Brief Chronology of China up to the Qing Dynasty

Paleolithic Period		600,000 to 10,000 years ago
Neolithic Period		10,000 to 4,000 years ago
Xia Dynasty		c. 21st-16th century B.C.
Shang Dynasty		c. 16th-11th century B.C.
Western Zhou Dynasty		11th century to 771 B.C.
Eastern Zhou Dynasty	Spring and Autumn Period	770-476 B.C.
	Warring States	475-221 B.C.
Qin Dynasty		221-207 B.C.
Han Dynasty	Western Han	206 B.C. - 23 A.D.
	Eastern Han	25-220
Three Kingdoms	Wei	220-265
	Shu Han	221-263
	Wu	222-280
Western Jin Dynasty		265-316
Period of Eastern Jin and Sixteen States	Eastern Jin Dynasty	317-420
	Sixteen States	304-439
Northern and Southern Dynasties	Southern Dynasties	
	Song	420-479
	Qi	479-502
	Liang	502-557
	Chen	557-589
	Northern Dynasties	
	Northern Wei	386-534
	Eastern Wei	534-550
	Western Wei	535-557
	Northern Qi	550-577
	Northern Zhou	557-581
Sui Dynasty		581-618
Tang Dynasty		618-907
Five Dynasties and Ten States	Five Dynasties	
	Later Liang	907-923
	Later Tang	923-936
	Later Jin	936-947
	Later Han	947-950
	Later Zhou	951-960
	Ten States	902-979
Song Dynasty	Northern Song Dynasty	960-1127
	Southern Song Dynasty	1127-1279
Liao Dynasty		916-1125
Western Xia Dynasty		1038-1227
Jin Dynasty		1115-1234
Yuan Dynasty		1271-1368
Ming Dynasty		1368-1644
Qing Dynasty		1644-1911

Chronology of Major Events in Ancient Chinese Architecture

Paleolithic Period

500,000 years ago	site of cave dwellings of the Peking Man in Longgu Shan, Zhoukou Dian, Beijing

Neolithic Period

5000 B.C.	site of ancient architecture revealing timber structure built with mortise and tenon joints in Hemudu, Yuyao, Zhejiang Province
3600 B.C.	site of a village of subterranean buildings in Banpo, Xi'an, Shaanxi Province and in Jiangyan Village, Lintong
3000 B.C.	site of a dwelling compound consisting of four houses in Dahe Village, Zhengzhou, Henan Province

Xia Dynasty (ca. 21st-16th century B.C.)

2000 B.C.	ruins of the city wall in Xiaxian, Shanxi Province

Shang Dynasty (ca. 16th-11th century B.C.)

1590-1300 B.C.	site of an early Shang palace in Yanshi, Henan Province
1400 B.C.	site of a Shang city wall of tamped earth construction in Zhengzhou, Henan
1300 B.C.	site of a middle Shang city and palace in Panlong City, Huangpo
ca. 1115 B.C.	site of a Shang ancestral temple, palace and cemetry in Xiaotun, Anyang, Henan

Western Zhou (ca. 11th century-771 B.C.)

1066 B.C.	Gaojing (near present-day Xi'an, Shaanxi) became new capital of the Western Zhou Dynasty
1063 B.C.	construction of Luoyang City or Chengzhou (present-day Luoyang City in Henan)
1024-1005 B.C.	the appearance of corbel brackets (*dou*) in Chinese architecture as evidenced by inscriptions on bronze sacrificial vessels of the time
ca. 1000 B.C.	site of a timber structure in Qichun, Hubei

Spring and Autumn Period (ca. 770-476 B.C.)

691-679 B.C.	State of Yan moved its capital to Linyi and renamed it Xiadu, the Lower Capital (south of present-day Yixian, Hebei Province)
689 B.C.	State of Chu built its capital at Ying (present-day Jinan City in Jingzhou, Hubei)
631-591 B.C.	State of Chu constructed the Shaopo (south of present-day Shouxian, Anhui Province)
585 B.C.	State of Jin moved its capital to Xintian (present-day Houma City, Shanxi)
541 B.C.	the first pontoon bridge constructed at the upper course of the Yellow River between the states of Qin and Jin
ca. 500 B.C.	huge timber coffin appeared in Xingyang, Henan
	lacquered timber wares popular as evidenced by recent excavations
	mining well with timber framework appeared in Tonglu Shan in Hubei during the late Autumn and Spring Period
486 B.C.	State of Wu cut the Han Canal which ran from Yangzhou to Huai'an, linking the Yangtze and Huai rivers

Warring States Period (475-221 B.C.)

475-221 B.C.	the *Kaogongji* (*The Artificers' Record*), a record of all technical knowledge of the time on craft and art as well as architecture, published
	images of terraces and pavilions inscribed on bronze wares of the period
	wells with clay walls appeared in Beijing
400 B.C.	Ximen Pao dug twelve canals in Ye City (present-day Lingzhang in Hebei) to channel the water from River Zhang for irrigation
386 B.C.	State of Qin made Liyang (north of present-day Lintong, Shaanxi) its capital
359 B.C.	State of Wei started building the west part of the Great Wall
351 B.C.	State of Qi built its portion of the Great Wall
350-207 B.C.	State of Qin constructed the Xinyang Palace on a high terrace
349 B.C.	State of Qin moved its capital to Xianyang
333 B.C.	State of Zhao built its portion of the Great Wall
266-255 B.C.	State of Qin built wood plank roads to Sichuan Province

	260 B.C.	State of Yan built the portion of Great Wall from Zaoyang to Xiangping
	257 B.C.	State of Qin constructed the Puzhou pontoon bridge over the Yellow River
	250 B.C.	Li Bing, an official of the State of Qin, reconstructed the Dujiang Weir (in present-day Guanxian)
	246 B.C.	State of Qin dug the Zhengguo Canal
	221 B.C.	State of Qin built the Great Wall from Lintao in the west to Liaodong in the east
Qin Dynasty (221-207 B.C.)		
	221 B.C.	palaces in imitation of the palaces of the six states in the east (namely, Qi, Chu, Yan, Han, Zhao, and Wei during the Warring States Period) built in Beiban, Xianyang
	221-209 B.C.	construction of the Mausoleum of the First Emperor of Qin in Lishan (present-day Lintong)
	220 B.C.	construction of highways, the bridge over the portion of River Wei in Xianyang, and the Xing Palace in Weinan
	214 B.C.	construction of the Ling Canal (in present-day Xing'an, Guangxi Province), linking the Yangtze River with the Pearl River
	212 B.C.	construction of the Epang Palace (at the southern bank of River Wei, Xianyang), thoroughfares and 270 palaces and temples 200 *li* (one *li* at that time is about 400 meters) around Xianyang
	206 B.C.	Xiang Yu occupied Xianyang and set fire to the Qin palaces which burnt for over three months
Han Dynasty (206 B.C.-220 A.D.)		
	202 B.C.	founding of Chang'an City (present-day Xi'an, Shaanxi) which became capital in 201 B.C.
	200 B.C.	construction of the city wall of Chang'an and building of the Changle Palace on the foundation of the Qin Xingle Palace
	199 B.C.	construction work of the Weiyang Palace began in 199 B.C. and completed in 198 B.C.
	179-158 B.C.	erection of the Baoxie Path (a wood plank road linking River Bao region with River Xie region in the Shaanxi Province)
	138 B.C.	construction of the Shanglin Garden (in present-day Xi'an, Shaanxi)
	130 B.C.	building of the Nanyi Road
	129 B.C.	the Cao Canal dug, linking River Wei in Chang'an with the Yellow River in Tong Guan
	120 B.C.	construction of the Kunming Lake southwest of Chang'an
	117 B.C.	erection of the Tomb of Huo Qubing (in Xingping, Shaanxi)
	ca. 113 B.C.	a large cave tomb of 2,700 cubic meters (subsequent archaeological designation Han Tomb number one), constructed in Mancheng, Hebei
	109 B.C.	erection of the Tongtian Terrace in Ganquan
	104 B.C.	construction of the Jianzhang Palace in western Chang'an
	102 B.C.	garrison stations built in Wuyuan, Juyan and other places along the Great Wall
	101 B.C.	construction of the Mingguang Palace in Chang'an
	37-32 B.C.	a funerary chamber with a square base and a domed brick ceiling constructed in Luoyang
	3 A.D.	construction of an imperial lecture and ceremonial hall (*mingtang*) and an imperial academy (*biyong*) in Chang'an
	20 A.D.	construction of the imperial ancestral temples (totaling nine) — *jiumiao* — in southern Chang'an
	36 A.D.	erection of the Li Ye Memorial Stone Archway (in Zitong, Sichuan Province)
	50 A.D.	construction of the stone Zhu Wei Memorial Temple (in Jinxiang, Shandong Province)
	56 A.D.	construction of an observatory (*lingtai*), an imperial academy and an imperial lecture and ceremonial hall in southern Luoyang
	65 A.D.	the Northern Palace (Bei Gong) in Luoyang completed
	68 A.D.	construction of the White Horse Temple (Baima Si) in Luoyang
	118 A.D.	erection of the Taishi Stone Archway (in Dengfeng, Henan)
	121 A.D.	erection of the Feng Huan Memorial Stone Archway (in Quxian, Sichuan)

122-125 A.D.	construction of the Shen Fujun Memorial Stone Archway (in Quxian)
129 A.D.	construction of the stone Gu Ju Memorial Temple (in Feicheng, Shandong)
147 A.D.	erection of the Wushi Stone Archway (Jiaxiang, Shandong)
170 A.D.	building of the Shangfu Pavilion in Yinping Dao (Lüeyang, Shaanxi)
193-195 A.D.	Ze Rong constructed many Buddhist temples in Guangling (present-day Yangzhou, Jiangsu)
209 A.D.	erection of the Gao Yi Memorial Stone Archway (Ya'an, Sichuan)
210-213 A.D.	Cao Cao ordered the construction of the Tongque, Jinfeng and Bingjing terraces in Ye Du (present-day Linzhang, Hebei)
212 A.D.	Sun Quan, king of the State of Wu, moved his capital to Jianye (present-day Nanjing) and ordered the construction of Shitou Cheng, the Stone City

Three Kingdoms Period (220-265 A.D.)

220 A.D.	Cao Pi created with stone of different colors the artificial hill of Jingyang in the Fragrant Wood Garden (Fanglin Yuan)
234 A.D.	Zhuge Liang, the celebrated prime minister of the State of Shu, erected bamboo bridges in Weinan, Wugong District, Shaanxi Province
235 A.D.	construction of the Luoyang Palace
ca. 240 A.D.	a brick tomb chamber, with its base joining its domed top at an angle of 45°, appeared in the South
247 A.D.	construction of the Taichu Palace

Western Jin Dynasty (265-316 A.D.)

274 A.D.	a pontoon bridge erected over the Yellow River in Mengjin, Henan
282 A.D.	the earliest stone arch bridge, the Travelers Bridge (Luren Qiao), erected in Qili Jian east of Luoyang
297 A.D.	construction of the Tomb of Zhou Chu (Yixing, Jiangsu Province)

Eastern Jin Dynasty (317-420 A.D.)

335 A.D.	State of Later Zhao moved its capital to Ye Cheng (present-day Linzhang) and constructed the city wall with brick
353-366 A.D.	construction work of the Mogao Grottoes at Dunhuang begun
372 A.D.	erection of a three-story Buddhist pagoda at the Changqian Temple in Jiankang
398 A.D.	State of Northern Wei moved its capital to Ping Cheng (Datong, Shanxi) and constructed palaces there
413 A.D.	State of Xia founded its capital at Tongwan Cheng (present-day Hengshan, Shaanxi)

Northern and Southern Dynasties Period (420-581 A.D.)

420-589 A.D.	buildings with heated brick beds constructed in Ji'an, Jilin Province
	glazed tiles appeared in Datong (Shanxi) and Nanjing (Jiangsu)
460-524 A.D.	State of Northern Wei started working on the Yungan Grottoes (Datong, Shanxi)
467 A.D.	Northern Wei erected the seven-story Pagoda of Yongling Temple in the capital Ping Cheng
493 A.D.	Northern Wei moved its capital to Luoyang
494-495 A.D.	Northern Wei started working on the Longmen Grottoes in Yique Shan in Luoyang
500-523 A.D.	Northern Wei opened up three caves at Binyang in Longmen
513 A.D.	Northern Wei constructed the Grotto of Bingling Temple
516 A.D.	Northern Wei built the nine-story wooden pagoda of Yongning Temple in Luoyang
521 A.D.	State of Liang constructed the Tongtai Temple in Jiankang
523 A.D.	Northern Wei built the brick pagoda of Xongyue Temple (Dengfeng, Henan)
524 A.D.	Northern Wei built a seven-story pagoda at Jingming Temple in Luoyang
534 A.D.	the Yongning Pagoda in Luoyang destroyed by lightning
	Eastern Wei moved its capital to Ye Cheng and constructed the new city Ye Nan Cheng
537 A.D.	the technique of *yunyan* applied to paintings at the Yicheng Temple in Danyang,

		producing an embossed appearance when viewed from a distance. *(Yunyan:* to bleed shading colors into a wet surface as in Chinese painting)
	547 A.D.	Yang Xuanzhi wrote the *Luoyang Qielan Ji (A Record of Buddhist Temples in Luoyang)* which provides much information on ancient Chinese architecture
	567-570 A.D.	erection of the Yi Ciwei Memorial Stone Column
Sui Dynasty (581-618 A.D.)		
	582-583 A.D.	construction of the Daxing City at the site southeast of the Han City Chang'an
	584-610 A.D.	excavation of the 1,794 kilometer Grand Canal (Da Yunhe), linking Zhuo County with Hangzhou
	589-608 A.D.	Li Chun constructed the Anji Bridge (also called the Grand Stone Bridge—Da Shiqiao) in Zhaoxian, Hebei
	595 A.D.	construction of the Renshou Palace
	601-604 A.D.	Yuwen Kai devised the wooden model of the Sui imperial lecture and ceremonial hall at a scale of 1 to 100
		the Sui Court sent to different provinces ashes of the Buddha and detailed plans of stupas and ordered the construction of stupas to house the ashes
	605-606 A.D.	construction of the East Capital (Dong Du) in the site south of Luoyang City of the Han and Wei dynasties
	605 A.D.	construction of Hanjialun City north of Luoyang
		erection of the Tianjin Pontoon Bridge over the River Luo and in which iron chains used to tie together the pontoon-boats to form the bridge
	607 A.D.	construction of the Jinyang Palace in Taiyuan
	611 A.D.	building of the Simen Pagoda of Shengtong Temple (in Licheng, Shandong)
Tang Dynasty (618-907 A.D.)		
	618 A.D.	the Sui Daxing City renamed Chang'an, expanded again and again in later years
	637-649 A.D.	construction of the Zhao Ling (Tomb of Emperor Taizong) in Liquan, Shaanxi
	652 A.D.	construction of the Dayan Pagoda of Ci'en Temple in Chang'an City; the pagoda later expanded to seven stories
	654 A.D.	the outer wall of Chang'an City built
	662-663 A.D.	construction of the Penglai Palace in the Longshou Plain northeast of Chang'an, renamed Daming Palace in 670 A.D.
	669 A.D.	construction of the Xuan Zhuang Pagoda of Xingjiao Temple (in Chang'an), refurbished in 828 A.D.
	672-679 A.D.	construction of the Statue of Buddha Mahāvairocana and the Fengxian Temple in Longmen, Luoyang
	681 A.D.	the Pagoda of the Xiangji Temple built
	688 A.D.	the Qianyuan Temple reconstructed into an imperial lecture and ceremonial hall and called the Wanxiang Shengong
	690 A.D.	imperial edicts issued to order the construction of a Dayun Temple in every province as well as at the East and West capitals
	691 A.D.	the Heavenly Hall (Tiantang) constructed at the back of the Luoyang Imperial Lecture and Ceremonial Hall to house the image of the Buddha
	707-709 A.D.	construction of the Xiaoyan Pagoda of the Jianfu Temple in Chang'an
	714 A.D.	construction of the Xingqing Palace in Chang'an
	715 A.D.	carving work on the Thousand Buddha Carved Cliff (Qianfo Yan Moyan) in Guanyuan, Sichuan
	732 A.D.	construction of the east double rampart walls (*jiacheng*) of Chang'an
	741–742 A.D.	excavation of the Xinmen Canal at the Sanmenxia City south of the Yellow River
	746 A.D.	erection of the Memorial Pagoda of the Monk Jingzang in Dengfeng, Henan
	756 A.D.	the Longquan Fu in Shangjing was constructed
	782 A.D.	construction of the main hall of the Zanchan Temple in Wutai, Shanxi

ca. 700–800 A.D.	the Qianxun Pagoda of Chongsheng Temple built in Dali, Yunnan Province
857 A.D.	construction of the East Main Hall of the Foguang Temple in Wutai, Shanxi
877 A.D.	the Memorial Pagoda of the Monk Minghui constructed
890–893 A.D.	Zhu Zundu wrote the *Qijing* (*A Classic of Lacquer*)

Five Dynasty (907-960 A.D.)

910 A.D.	State of Wuyue constructed the Hanhai Stone Pool
917 A.D.	State of Wuyue erected the Nine-storied Pagoda of Asoka (Ayuwang) Temple
918 A.D.	State of Former Shu constructed the Yong Ling (Tomb of Wang Jian) in Chengdu, Sichuan
937-975 A.D.	State of Later Jin erected the Sheli Stupa (Stupa for the Buddha's Ashes) of the Jinxia Temple
907-960 A.D.	construction of the Twin Stone Pagodas of Linyin Temple (Hangzhou, Zhejiang Province)
955 A.D.	State of Later Zhou reconstructed the Bianliang City in Kaifeng, Henan
959 A.D.	State of Later Zhou constructed the Pagoda of Yunyan Temple in Suzhou, Jiangsu Province

Northern Song Dynasty (960-1127 A.D.)

960 A.D.	Chen Xiliang built the Suzhou Flying Bridge without column support
962 A.D.	extension of the Dongjing Cheng or East Capital (present-day Kaifeng, Henan), utilizing the palaces in Luoyang as a model
963 A.D.	State of Northern Han constructed the Wanfo Hall (Ten Thousand Buddha Hall) of Zhenguo Temple in Pingyao, Shanxi
964 A.D.	construction of the main hall of Hualin Temple in Fuzhou, Fujian Province
970 A.D.	construction of the eave of Cave 427 of the Mogao Grottoes in Dunhuang
971 A.D.	construction of the Foxiang Pavilion and erection of the 24 meter Guangyin (Avalokitesvara) Statue in Longxin Temple (Zhengding, Hebei)
975 A.D.	construction of the Leifeng Pagoda in Hangzhou, Zhejiang
976 A.D.	construction of the eave of Cave 444 of the Mogao Grottoes in Dunhuang
977 A.D.	the Longhua Pagoda (in Shanghai) built
980 A.D.	construction of the eave of Cave 431 of the Mogao Grottoes
982 A.D.	construction of the Twin Pagodas of Lohan (Arhat) Temple in Suzhou, Jiangsu Province
984 A.D.	State of Liao constructed the Guanyin Pavilion of Dule Temple
989 A.D.	the famous architect, Yu Hao, constructed the Wooden Pagoda of Kaibao Temple in Dongjing (present-day Kaifeng, Henan) and wrote the three volume *Mu Jing* (*Classic of Wood*) which no longer exists
1001-1055 A.D.	construction of the Liaodi Pagoda of Kaiyuan Temple (Zhengding, Henan)
1066 A.D.	the Houtu Temple built in Fenyin (Wanrong, Shanxi)
1008-1014 A.D.	construction of the Yuqing Zhaoying Palace in Dongjing, the East Capital (Kaifeng, Henan)
1016 A.D.	construction of the Sanqing Hall of Xuanmiao Temple (Putian, Fujian)
1020 A.D.	State of Liao constructed the main hall of Fengguo Temple in Yixian, Liaoning Province
1023-1032 A.D.	construction of the Shengmu Hall of the Jin Ancestral Temple (Taiyuan, Shanxi)
1038 A.D.	State of Liao constructed the Library of Bhagavad Sūtras of the Xia Huayan Temple in Xijing, the West Capital (present-day Datong) and the Dhâranî Sūtra Stele in Zhaoxian, Hebei
1044 A.D.	Shen Li completed his work *Hefang Tongyi* (*A Treatise on Controlling the Yellow River*)
1052 A.D.	construction of the Muni (Śākaymuni) Hall of Longxing Temple in Zhengding, Hebei
1053-1059 A.D.	construction of Wan'an Bridge, also called the Luoyang Bridge, in Hui'an, Fujian
1056 A.D.	State of Liao constructed the Xijia (Śākaymuni) Pagoda of Fogong Temple in Yingxian, Shanxi
1072 A.D.	Shen Kuo studied the Bian River, surveyed the topography and built coffer dams layer by layer

1075 A.D.		completion of the *Xiucheng Fashi* (*Standard Methods in City Building*), with Shen Kuo as the chief editor
		the coffer dam of Mulanpo constructed under the direction of Shen Kuo
1075-1078 A.D.		repairing of the city wall of Dongjing (East Capital), using simple scurrying roller for the first time
1089 A.D.		State of Liao constructed the Pagoda of Jueshan Temple in Lingqiu, Shanxi
1094-1099 A.D.		people in Huizhou channeled spring water into town with bamboo pipes
1097-1100 A.D.		Li Jie compiled the *Yingzao Fashi* (*Treatise on Architectural Methods*), made the official guidebook in 1103 A.D.
11th century A.D.		construction of the main hall of Baoguo Temple in Ningbo, Zhejiang
		construction of the Zhuanlunzang Hall of Longxing Temple (Zhengding, Hebei)
1102 A.D.		the Grand Buddhist Hall of Qinglian Temple constructed in Jincheng, Shanxi
1114 A.D.		erection of the Tianjin Bridge in Luoyang
1117-1122 A.D.		construction of the Wanshou Shan, also called Gen Yue, in the East Capital
1124 A.D.		State of Jin constructed the main hall of Jingtu Temple
1125 A.D.		construction of the Chuzao Nunnery of Shaolin Temple in Dengfeng, Henan

Southern Song Dynasty (1127-1279 A.D.)

1131-1162 A.D.		construction of the Pagoda of Bao'en Temple, also called the Pagoda of the North Temple
1137 A.D.		the Jin Dynasty (1115-1234 A.D.) in the North constructed the Wenshu Hall of Foguang Temple in Wutai, Shanxi
1138 A.D.		the Southern Song Dynasty chose Lin'an in Hangzhou, Zhejiang, as its capital
1138-1151 A.D.		erection of the 2070 meter long Anping Bridge
1140 A.D.		the Jin Dynasty constructed the Mituo (Amitabha) Hall of Chongfu Temple
1145 A.D.		Wang Huan reprinted the *Yingzao Fashi* (*Treatise on Architectural Methods*) in Pingjiang (Suzhou, Jiangsu)
11th-12th century		construction of the Shanhua Temple in Datong, Shanxi by the Liao and Jin dynasties
1151 A.D.		Yuanyan Liang, Emperor of the Jin Dynasty, started the construction of Yanjing (present-day Beijing) which was renamed Zhongdu — the Central Capital — in 1153
1153-1163 A.D.		construction of the Liuhe Pagoda on Mount Yuelun in Hangzhou, Zhejiang
1167 A.D.		murals depicting stories of the Buddha painted on the inner wall of the main hall of Lingyan Temple in Fanshi, Shanxi under the reign of the Jin Dynasty
1168 A.D.		the Jin Dynasty constructed the Sacrificial House of Shengmu Hall in the Jin Ancestral Temple (Taiyuan, Shanxi)
1169 A.D.		construction of the folding bridge of Guangji in Chaozhou, Guangdong Province
1170 A.D.		reconstructed the city wall of Hexian in Anhui, using a mixture of glutinous rice and lime for cementing
1179 A.D.		construction of the Sanqing Hall of Xuanmiao Temple (Suzhou, Jiangsu)
1192 A.D.		the Jin Dynasty completed the construction of Lugou Qiao (Marco Polo Bridge) which began in 1189
1195 A.D.		the Jin Dynasty constructed the Bei Ting (Steles Pavilion) of the Confucius Temple in Qufu, Shandong
12th century A.D.		construction of the Guang Ta of Huisheng Temple (*Guang Ta* originally a phonetic rendering of the minaret's Islamic name, could also refer to lights mounted on top and to its reflecting plain surface)
1229 A.D.		stone inscription of the layout of Pingjiang (Suzhou, Jiangsu) carved
1237-1240 A.D.		erection of the Jiangdong Bridge in Zhangzhou, Fujian
1237-1250 A.D.		construction of the Twin Pagodas of Kaiyuan Temple
1252-1262 A.D.		the Mongolian Empire expanded the Chunyang Wanshou Palace, also called the Yongle Palace (the palace originally situated at Yongji in Shanxi, but in 1959 removed to Ruicheng in the same province)
1256 A.D.		the Mongolian Empire built its capital at Shangdu Cheng (present-day Dolonnur in Inner

Mongolia)

Yuan Dynasty (1271-1368 A.D.)

1267-1274 A.D.	Kublai Khan constructed the Grand Capital — Dadu Cheng (present-day Beijing)
1272 A.D.	map of Guizhou City inscribed on a cliff
1279 A.D.	construction of an observatory, the Guanxing Tai, in Dengfeng, Henan
1281 A.D.	construction of the main hall of Fenghuang (Phoenix) Temple in Hangzhou
1284 A.D.	construction of the North Temple of Chongguo in the Grand Capital — Dadu (present-day Huguo Temple in Beijing)
1289 A.D.	excavation of the Huitong River from Shouzhang to Linqing in Shandong Province
mid 13th century A.D.	construction of the Sa'gya Temple in Tibet
1306 A.D.	construction of the Ciyun Pavilion in Dingxing, Hebei
1309 A.D.	construction of the main hall of the Lower Temple of Guangsheng (Hongdong, Shanxi)
1318 A.D.	the main hall of Tianning Temple constructed
1320 A.D.	construction of the main hall of Zhengru Temple
1321 A.D.	Sha Keshi completed his *Hefang Tongyi* (*Treatise on Controlling the Yellow River*)
1322 A.D.	reconstruction of the Wanshou Bridge over the Min River in Fuzhou, Fujian
1324 A.D.	construction of Prince Mingying Palace in Hongdong, Shanxi
1333 A.D.	construction of the main hall of the Yong'an Temple (Langzhong, Sichuan)
1341-1368 A.D.	reconstruction of the Qingjing Temple (Quanzhou, Fujian)
1341-1367 A.D.	building of the Shizi Lin (Lion Rock Garden) of Suchou, Jiangsu
1345 A.D.	construction of the Cloud Terrace (Yun Tai) of the Juyong Guan (Changping, Beijing)
1363 A.D.	construction of Tulug Temür's Tomb (in Huocheng, Xinjiang)
1366 A.D.	Zhu Yuanzhang, the first Ming emperor, constructed palaces in Yingtian Fu (present-day Nanjing)

Ming Dynasty (1368-1644 A.D.)

1368 A.D.	Jinling made the capital and Yingtian Fu, where Jinling was situated, renamed Nanjing, the South Capital
	palaces of the Yuan capital of Dadu demolished and the north city wall reduced by five *li* (one Ming *li* is about 570 meters)
1369 A.D.	the Ming dynasty made Linhao (present-day Fengyang in Anhui Province) the Central Capital (Zhongdu) and city walls as well as palaces built there
1372 A.D.	construction of the Garrison City of Jiayu Guan (Jiuquan, Gansu), refurbished and expanded in 1539
1373 A.D.	construction of the city and palaces of Nanjing completed
1376-1382 A.D.	the main hall of Linggu Temple constructed (Nanjing)
1381-1383 A.D.	construction of the Xiao Ling (tomb of the first Ming emperor, Zhu Yuanzhang) in Zhongshan, Nanjing
1387 A.D.	fifty-nine border towns and garrison cities built along the coasts
1390 A.D.	construction of the Mosque in Huajie Lane in Xi'an
14th century	construction of the Atikar Mosque
1407 A.D.	construction of palaces in Beijing, the North Capital
1409 A.D.	construction of the Ming tombs in Tianshou Mountain, Changping District, began; the first and greatest tomb, Chang Ling (tomb of Emperor Yong Le), completed in 1415 with the passage to the tombs completed in 1435
1412-1418 A.D.	construction of the temples in Wudang Mountain, Hubei
1412-1431 A.D.	reconstruction of the Pagoda of Bao'en Temple in Nanjing
1416 A.D.	construction of the Bronze Temple (Tong Dian) of Wudang Mountain
	construction work of the West Palace (Xi Gong) to the west of Taiye Lake in Beijing began in 1416 and completed in 1417
1417 A.D.	construction of the imperial palace city and residences of the ten princes in Beijing
1419 A.D.	the southern city of Beijing expanded by one *li* (0.57 kilometer)

1420 A.D.	the palace city and imperial residence completed and the capital moved into Beijing construction of the Temple of Heaven (Tian Tan), repaired twice in 1530 and 1751 with its Qinian Temple rebuilt in 1896
1421 A.D.	the inner city of Beijing completed in 1421 with the outer city finished in 1553
1439 A.D.	construction of the Fahai Temple in Beijing
1444 A.D.	construction of the Zhihua Temple in Beijing
1445 A.D.	erection of the Jade Belt (Yudai) Bridge in Suzhou, Jiangsu
1447 A.D.	construction of the Trashilungpo Monastery in Xigazê
1452 A.D.	the Longfu Temple in Beijing built
1473 A.D.	construction of the Buddha's Seat (Jingan Baozuo) Pagoda of Zhenjue Temple (also called the Pagoda of Five Pagodas Temple) in Beijing
1497 A.D.	the Junji Hall of Zhongyue Temple on Song Mountain completed
15th century A.D.	repairing of the Great Wall
1504 A.D.	the Confucius Temple (Qufu, Shandong), constructed in the Han Dynasty, made as grand in scale as ever
1506-1510 A.D.	the Jichang Garden in Wuxi constructed, subsequently destroyed in 1860 and later repaired
1515-1527 A.D.	construction of the Feihong Pagoda of Guangsheng Temple (Hongdong, Shanxi)
1522-1566 A.D.	the Zhuozheng Garden in Suzhou built
1530 A.D.	construction of the Huangqiu Altar within the Temple of Heaven in Beijing
1531 A.D.	construction of the Lidai Diweng Miao (Temple for Emperors Throughout the Ages)
1534 A.D.	construction of the Shenyu Pavilion, i.e. the Imperial Archive (Huangshi Cheng), began in 1534 and ended in 1536
1539 A.D.	the Huanqiong House of the Temple of Heaven constructed
1544 A.D.	reconstruction of the Imperial Ancestral Temple in Beijing
1559-1577 A.D.	construction of the Yu Garden and the Nei Garden in Shanghai, both of which refurbished in 1760
1576 A.D.	construction of Pagoda of Cishou Temple
16th century	the library of Tianyi Pavilion constructed
	Pan Jixun wrote the *Hefang Yilan* (*On Controlling the Yellow River*)
1603 A.D.	construction of the Beamless Hall (Wuliang Dian) of Kaiyuan Temple in Suzhou
1615 A.D.	reconstruction of the Jianji Hall (Baohe Hall) in the palace city of Beijing
1627 A.D.	reconstruction of the Zhongji Hall (Zhonghe Hall) in the Beijing palace city
1634 A.D.	Ji Cheng wrote the 3 volume *Yuan Ye* (*Garden-making*)
1637 A.D.	Song Yingxing wrote the 18 volume *Tiangong Kaiwu* (*Exploitation of the Works of Nature*, an important book on industrial technology of the time)
1643 A.D.	the Qing Dynasty constructed the Zhao Ling (tomb of Emperor Tai Zong of Qing) in Shengjing (the Magnificent Capital), Shenyang, Liaoning

Qing Dynasty (1644-1911 A.D.)

1644 A.D.	the Qing Dynasty moved its capital to Beijing
1645 A.D.	construction of the Potala Palace in Lhasa, Tibet
1655 A.D.	reconstruction of the Qianqing Palace in the Beijing palace city
1663 A.D.	construction work of the Dong Ling (East Tombs) in Junhua, Hebei, began
1665 A.D.	erection of the Puji Bridge in Xi'an, the technique used in its construction being applied again when the three bridges of Ba, Chan and Feng were built
1667 A.D.	reconstruction of the Duan Gate of Beijing palace city
1669 A.D.	construction of the White Pagoda (Bai Ta) in the West Garden (Xi Yuan) in Beijing
1672 A.D.	Li Yu wrote the *Yijia Yan* (*One Man's View*, which contains Li Yu's observations on art and building)
1680 A.D.	the Ministry of Work constructed glazing kilns in Beijing
1689 A.D.	construction of the Changchun Garden in the western suburb of Beijing

1690 A.D.	reconstruction of the Taihe Palace in the palace city of Beijing, the whole work completed in 1695
1691 A.D.	construction of the Huizong Temple in Dolonnur, Inner Mongolia
1692 A.D.	the Chengxin Garden in Yuquan Mountain rebuilt and renamed the Jinming Garden
	construction of the Xiangshan Imperial Traveling Lodge
1696 A.D.	construction of the Shireetu Dzuu in Hohhot, Inner Mongolia
1701 A.D.	erection of the Luding Bridge, also called the Tiesuo (Iron Chain) Bridge, in Luding, Sichuan
1702 A.D.	construction of the Wangshan Imperial Traveling Lodge in Beijing, later renamed the Qingyi Garden. It again changed its name to Yihe Garden in subsequent years while to Westerners it known as the Summer Palace. In 1860, the garden destroyed by the Anglo-French expedition and repaired two times in 1888 and 1903
1703-1708 A.D.	construction of the Imperial Summer Resort in Rehe (Chengde, Hebei)
1704 A.D.	reconstruction of the Huanghe (Yellow Crane) Mansion in Wuchang, Hubei
1709 A.D.	construction of the Yuanming Garden (The garden demolished in 1860 by the Anglo-French expedition)
	construction of the Labrang Monastery (Xiahe, Gansu)
1723 A.D.	construction of the Xihuang Temple in Beijing
1725 A.D.	reconstruction of the Grand Buddhist Hall in Fengping (Luxi, Yunnan)
1727 A.D.	the Cideng Temple built in Hohhot, Inner Mongolia
1730 A.D.	construction of the Xi Ling (West Tombs) in Yixian, Hebei
1734 A.D.	*Gongcheng Zuofa Zeli* (*Standard Rules on Construction*) compiled by the Ministry of Work. Published in 1936
1746 A.D.	construction of the Feiyun Mansion in Wanrong, Shanxi
1747 A.D.	construction in Yuanming Garden of a European fountain
1752 A.D.	reconstruction of the palaces in Shengjing (Shenyang, Liaoning)
1755 A.D.	construction of the Puning Temple in Rehe (Chengde, Hebei)
1764 A.D.	the Anyuan Temple built in Rehe
1766 A.D.	construction of the Pule Temple in Rehe
1767-1771 A.D.	construction of the Putuo Zongcheng Temple in Rehe
1774 A.D.	the Wenyuan Pavilion built in Beijing
1778 A.D.	construction of the Amin Pagoda and Worshipping Hall in Turpan, Xinjiang
1779-1780 A.D.	construction of the Xumi (Sumeru) Fushou Temple
1784 A.D.	construction of the Qingjing Huacheng Pagoda of Xihuang Temple in Beijing
1793 A.D.	publication of the *Qinding Gongbu Zeli* (*Imperial Standard Rules of the Ministry of Work*)
1796-1820 A.D.	reconstruction of the Bihan Mountain Villa (also known as the Liu Garden) on its Ming Dynasty foundation
1796 A.D.	erection of the Anlan Bridge, also known as the Zhusuo (Bamboo Chain) Bridge, in Guanxian, Sichuan
18th century A.D.	construction of the Kumbum Temple (Huangzhong, Qinghai) and the Tombo of Appak Khodja (Kashi, Xinjiang)
1803 A.D.	reconstruction of the Wenchang Bridge in Linchuan, Jiangxi
1833-1834 A.D.	erection of the Ba Bridge in Xi'an, Shaanxi

Acknowlegements

The majority of the photographs in this album were taken by the Chinese Academy of Architecture. Others were loaned by various organizations and individuals listed below, to whom the Editors wish to express their thanks.

China Pictorial
Primitive man's dwelling, Beijing
Shanhai Guan
Jiayu Guan
Exterior view of Atikar Mosque
Luding Bridge
Houses of the Miao people in Rongshui

Institute of Archaeology, Chinese Academy of Sciences
Banpo archaeological site
Quadrangular house at Banpo archaeological site
Circular house at Banpo archaeological site
Erlitou archaeological site
Reconstruction of Erlitou archaeological site
Archaeological site of Panlong City
Archaeological site of Western Zhou buildings
Ruins of a ritual building at Han Chang'an
Ruins of Xuanping Gate at Han Chang'an
Site of Mingde Gate
Site of Hanyuan Hall of Daming Palace

Zhengzhou Museum
Archaeological site at Dahe Village, Zhengzhou

Mr Luo Zhewen
Shang City archaeological site
Xiaotianping Spillway Dam at Ling Canal
Eastern Han colored burial article
Yi Ciwei Stone Memorial Column
Four Entrance Pagoda of Shentong Temple
Earthern house of the Sui Dynasty
Carvings 1-2 on the balustrades of Anji Bridge
Interior view of East Hall of Foguang Temple
Qianxun Pagoda of Chongsheng Temple
Ten Thousand Avatamsake Sutra Pagoda
Coffered ceiling in the hall of Jingtu Temple

Star Observation Platform
Cloud Terrace of Juyong Guan
Taihe Hall Square, Forbidden City
Jing Ling, Junhua
Mahayana Pavilion of Puning Temple
Lamaist Pavilion of Puning Temple
Wenchang Pavilion, Shanghang
Overhanging Temple, Hunyuan
Northern Gallery of Qionghua Island, Bei Hai Park
Yanyu Mansion of Imperial Summer Resort

Office of Foreign Exhibitions, State Administrative
Bureau of Museums and Archaeological Data
Bronze casing unearthed at Fengxiang, Shaanxi
Mural in a Han tomb in Horinger, Inner Mongolia

Palace Museum
Renmants of bronzewares of the Warring States
River Scene During Ching Ming Festival

Museum of Chinese History
Laomu Terrace, Site of Yan Xiadu
West wall of the outer city of Yan Xiadu
Gargoyle with a animal head
*   design discovered at Yan Xiadu*
Semi-cylindrical tile discovered at Yan Xiadu
Han brick with moulded design
*   discovered at Chengdu*

Exhibition Office, Ministry of Water Conservancy
Dujiang Weir

Cultural Hall of Lintong
Tile-end discovered at Mausoleum of
*   the First Emperor of Qin*

Chongqing Museum
Jun Watchtower at Pingyang Fu

Maiji Shan Storeroom of Cultural Relics
Panorama of Maiji Mountain

New China News Agency, Henan Branch
Pagoda of Songyue Monastery
Pagoda of Youguo Temple

State Administrative Bureau of Museums and
Archaeological Data
Mural in the tomb of Prince Yide
Central chamber of the underground hall of Ding Ling
Panorama of the Summer Palace

Xinjiang Uygur Autonomous Region Museum
Ruins of Gaochang City
Ruins of Jiaohe City
Tuglug Temur's Tomb
Amin Stupa and Worshipping Hall

Shanghai Museum
Painting of a hydraulic mill of the Five Dynasties

Picture Center of China
Drum Tower and Bell Tower, Beijing
Bird's-eye view of Temple of Heaven

Photographic Studio, Foreign Languages Press
Coffered ceiling in Taihe Hall, Forbidden City
Taihe Men, Forbidden City
Stone memorial archway of
*   the Thirteen Mausoleums of Ming*
Animal statues at the Thirteen Mausoleums
*Brilliant Tower (*Minglou*) on Square Gatehouse*
*   (*Fangcheng*) of Chang Ling*
Nine Dragon Wall, Bei Hai Park

Photographic Studio, Internal Section,
New China News Agency
Panorama of Potala Palace
Trashilungpo Monastery
Yinping Bridge
Norbu Liangka

New China News Agency, Hebei Branch
Hall of the Mansion on Bridge, Jingxing

253

26/7/82
320 Nott

CANCELLED

UNIVERSITY
OXFORD
COLLEGE

UNIVERSITY OXFORD COLLEGE